FOOTFALLS OF INDIAN HISTORY

FOOTFALLS OF INDIAN HISTORY

THE SISTER NIVEDITA

WITH 6 PLATES
AND 22 OTHER ILLUSTRATIONS

GYAN

Published by

GYAN

Gyan Publishing House
5, Ansari Road
Daryaganj, New Delhi-110002
Phone: 011-47034999, 9811692060
E-mail: books@gyanbooks.com

Distribution Network
gyanbooks.com
India, USA, Canada, UK, Australia, France

ISBN : 978-81-212-9622-9 (PB)
First Published, 1915

2nd Impression 2023

Printed at: Gyan Press, Delhi.

FOOTFALLS OF INDIAN HISTORY
Author: THE SISTER NIVEDITA

FOOTFALLS OF INDIAN HISTORY

BY

THE SISTER NIVEDITA

(MARGARET E. NOBLE)

AUTHOR OF

"THE WEB OF INDIAN LIFE," "THE MASTER AS I SAW HIM"
"STUDIES FROM AN EASTERN HOME," ETC.

WITH 6 PLATES
AND 22 OTHER ILLUSTRATIONS

1915

THE FOOTFALLS

We hear them, O Mother!
        Thy footfalls,
Soft, soft, through the ages
   Touching earth here and there,
And the lotuses left on Thy footprints
        Are cities historic,
Ancient scriptures and poems and temples,
   Noble strivings, stern struggles for Right.

Where lead they, O Mother!
        Thy footfalls?
O grant us to drink of their meaning!
   Grant us the vision that blindeth
   The thought that for man is too high.
Where lead they, O Mother!
        Thy footfalls?

Approach Thou, O Mother, Deliverer!
      Thy children, Thy nurslings are we!
   On our hearts be the place for Thy stepping,
      Thine own, Bhumia Devi, are we.
Where lead they, O Mother!
        Thy footfalls?

CONTENTS

ILLUSTRATIONS

PLATES

PLATES

FOOTFALLS OF INDIAN HISTORY

THE HISTORY OF MAN AS DETERMINED BY PLACE

THE character of a people is their history as written in their own subconscious mind, and to understand that character we have to turn on it the lime-light of their history. Then each anomaly is explained, and the whole becomes a clear and consistent result of causes traced to their very root. In the same way the geographical distribution of ideas falls under the same explanation as absolutely as that of plants or animals. A map of a country is only a script produced by all the ages of its making. In the beautiful maps of the past, in which rivers are seen with their true value as the high roads of nature, the veins and arteries of civilisations, this fact was still more apparent than to-day, when the outstanding lines of connection between cities are railways, the channels of the drainage of wealth being of more importance than those of its production. Yet even now it is the river-made cities that the railways have to connect. Even the twentieth century cannot escape the conditions imposed by the past.

Only the history of Asia explains the geography of Asia. Empire means organisation, organisation whose basis is the consciousness of a unity that transcends the family. That is to say, empire demands as its preceding condition a strong civic concept. Two types of empire have occurred within the last two thousand years: one the creation of the fisher-peoples of the European coast-line, the other of the tribesmen of Central Asia and Arabia. In the one case, the imperialising instinct is to be accounted for by the commercial thirst natural to those whose place has always been on the prehistoric trade-route. It may be true, as suggested by a distinguished scholar, that the salmon-fishery of Norway, with its tightly organised crew, giving birth to the pirate-fisher, the Viking, and he to the Norman, is to be regarded as the father of the Feudal System and immediate ancestor of all modern European Empire. Such considerations can, however, by no means account for the Roman Empire. To this it might be answered that behind Rome lay Greece and Carthage; behind Greece and Carthage, Phœnicia and Crete; and that here we come once more on the element of trade-routes and fisher-peoples. A strong sense of unity precedes aggression, and the sense of unity is made effective through internal definition and self-organisation. Such organisation is obviously easy to gain by the conquest of the sea, where captain, first mate, and second mate will be a father, with his eldest son and second son, and where the slightest dereliction from military discipline on the part of one may involve instant peril of death to all. Thus the family gives place, in the imagination, to the crew, as the organised unit of the human fabric, and the love of hearthside and brood becomes exalted into that civic passion which can offer up its seven sons and yet say with firm voice, "Sweet and seemly is it to die for one's country."

The second type of imperial organisation, seen within the last two thousand years, is the pastoral empire of Central Asia and Arabia. Islam was the religious form taken by the national unification of a number of pastoral tribes in Arabia. Mohammed, the Prophet of God, was in truth the greatest nation-maker who has ever appeared. The earliest associations of the Arabs are inwoven with the conception of the tribe as a civic unity, transcending the family unity; and the necessity of frontier-tribal relationships and courtesies at once suggests the idea of national inclusiveness, and creates a basis for national life. On these elements were laid the foundation of the thrones of Baghdad, Constantinople, and Cordova. The Hunnish, Scythic, and Mohammedan empires of India have, each in its turn, been offshoots from the nomadic organisations of Central Asia. The very name of the Moghul dynasty perpetuates its Tartar origin.

Here again, we see examples of the educational value of tribal and pastoral life, in preparing communities for the organisation of nations and empires.

In the far past, those shadowy empires whose memories are all but dead to man—the Assyrian, the Parthian, the Median, and some others—seem to have based their powers of aggression and co-operation on the instincts and associations of the hunter. From one point of view, the hunter is on land what the fisher is on water; and the soldier is only a hunter of men. But the mind of man is supreme. Even the results of a peculiar occupational education may be appropriated by others, through the intellect alone. In ancient Egypt the world saw a peasant nation stirred to emulation by the sight of empires—Hittite, Babylonian, Cretan, and perhaps Phœnician—and fully able to protect itself by its grasp of the idea of national solidarity and self-defence. This is the value of science, that it analyses a fact, displays the secret of power, and enables man to formulate new methods for arriving at the old result.

The sense of unity can only occur, as a spiritual reaction on the mind, against a manifoldness. Whether it be the cities of Egypt, the tribes of Arabia and Tartary, or the fleet of pirate vessels from many kindred harbours that give birth to this sense, it needs when born to be watched, trained, and guided in definite ways. The patriarch, deeply versed in strategy, must be still more experienced in the maintenance of intertribal peace. The men who unite, with the energy of the thunderbolt, for the attainment of the common goal of heart and conscience, must be men accustomed to combined action and sustained co-operation ; men who know the grounds of their faith in one another ; men who are familiar with certain outstanding principles of conduct, and constantly dominated by them. Such character, such experience, is built up for the service of the nation by social forms like those of tribe and crew and lion-hunt. The requisite discipline is conferred by the necessity of obedience on peril of death. The large outlook and due combination of readiness for war with love of peace are created by lifelong considerations of the common good and the way in which it is to be served by a clear mutual understanding. And all these results have been produced on mankind, unsought, by its history and its environment.

THE HISTORY OF INDIA AND ITS STUDY

I

India as she is is a problem which can only be read by the light of Indian history. Only by a gradual and loving study of how she came to be, can we grow to understand what the country actually is, what the intention of her evolution, and what her sleeping potentiality may be.

We are often told that Indian literature includes no histories. It is said that the *Rajatarangini* in Kashmir, the *Dipawaṃsa* and *Mahawamsa* in Ceylon, and the records made after their accession to power by the Mohammedans are the only real works of history which she possesses. Even if this be true—and we shall be better able to discuss the question in a generation or two—we must remember that India herself is the master-document in this kind. The country is her own record. She is the history that we must learn to read. There are those who say that history as a form of literature can never survive the loss of political power, and that this is the reason why India has not more works of an accurate and dynastic character. Those who urge this believe that at each new epoch in her history vast numbers of chronicles belonging to the past have been destroyed. May be. On the other hand, we may find in our family pedigrees the counterpart and compensation for this feature of other national literatures. The little band of devoted scholars who are already at work on the history of Bengal tell us that their great trouble is to keep pace with their material. It pours in upon them day after day. The difficulty is to keep to-day's opinion so fluid and receptive that it shall not conflict with, or be antagonistic to, to-morrow's added knowledge. There may not at the moment be in our inheritance from the past many formal works of history. But perhaps the swimmer, who knows the joy of the plunge into deep waters and strong currents, is glad. Such minds feel that they have abundance of material for the writing of history, and are thankful indeed that this has been left for them to do.

It will be from amongst the records of home and family-life that light will be shed upon the complete history of Bengal. It will be by searching into caste origins and tribal traditions that real data will be gathered for estimating the antiquity of processes. It is said that an overwhelming proportion of the higher-caste families of Bengal came from Magadha. If this be so, it is necessary to assume that there was at a certain time a wholesale evacuation of Magadha. This would agree so well with the facts of history—the removal of the capital to Gour, on the destruction of Pataliputra, and the immense cultural potentiality of the Bengali people—that the suggestion cannot fail to form a dominant note in subsequent research. Such research must for some time be of a deeply inductive character. That is to say, it will proceed by the accumulation of particulars. This process is the ideal of modern science, and it may be said that so arduous and so against the natural appetite of the human mind is it, that few there be that attain unto it. Yet as an ideal its greatness is unquestionable. Conclusions reached by careful gathering of facts without bias towards one or reaction against another theory are incontrovertible. For this reason anyone who can bring forward one fact out of the far past, however private or circumscribed may seem its significance, so long as it is unknown and certain, is doing a service to historians. For progress must for some time depend upon this accumulation. We must investigate the elements in order to come at true concepts of the whole.

When we have reached a new fact, the next effort should be to relate it to known central events. We know for instance that capitals changed in Bengal from Pataliputra to Gour, and from Gour to Vikrampur. These transitions could not take place without immense social consequences. The ruins of Behar mark the long struggle of Bengal against invasion. This fact belongs to her military history. But another record is found in her industrial development. The transfer of government from the old Hindu centre of Vikrampur to the Mohammedan capitals of Dacca and Murshidabad, meant, in its turn, great changes in the direction of arts and crafts. It would be marked by new tendencies in the matter of taste, the old artistic power exerting itself to meet new standards. We must accustom ourselves to the psychological analysis of ornament and the historical and geographical placing of works of art, in order to understand the immense influence of great political events upon private life and interests. Architecture, music, and poetry are things higher than the concrete industrial crafts of home and household life, yet marked, no less surely, with the era to which they belong. By learning to refer everything to its own time and to the state of mind that gave it birth, we build up in ourselves a wonderful readiness for the graver and more serious aspects of history. We learn too that lesson which botanists, zoologists, and geologists have had during the last century to learn and teach, namely, that things which are found together may have taken wide distances of space and time to produce. The poems of Vidyapati and Ram Mohun Roy may stand side by side in our hymn-books, but what travail of the human spirit lies between the making of the two! In ages of normal growth a new mode, in building, or graving, or thinking, is born but slowly, and goes much deeper than we can imagine in these degenerate days of trumpery and passing fashions. No one who has been in the Fort of Agra, and noted the styles of using black and white marble against red sandstone, distinctive of the reigns of Akbar, Jehangir, and Shah Jehan, could afterwards make a mistake as to which of these a particular pattern must be assigned to. The designs appear side by side at Agra, yet it took three reigns to make them possible.

The year, as we go through it, constitutes another kind of historical record. The festivals of the old village life which follow each other in such quick and delightful succession throughout the twelve or thirteen moons of the solar year, are not all effects of some single cause. On the contrary, the Car-festival of July hails from Buddhism, and has the great metropolis of its observance at Puri on the Orissan coast. But Janmashtami belongs to the Vaishnavism of Krishna, and turns our eyes in a very different direction, to Mathura and Brindaban. The Dewali Puja, again, connects us on the one side with the famous Japanese Feast of Lanterns, and on the other with Latin and Celtic anniversaries of the souls of the dead. How different are the thought-worlds out of which spring inspirations so various as all these! How long a period must each have had, in order to win its present depth and extent of influence! The very year as it passes, then, is a record of the changing ideas that have swept in succession across the Indian mind.

It is a characteristic of India that almost every great outstanding thought and doctrine has somewhere or other a place devoted to its maintenance and tradition. This brings us to the thought of the geographical synthesis. The whole of India is necessary to the explanation of the history of each one of its parts. The story of Krishna comes from the Jumna, that of Rama from Ayodhya. Other elements may not be so easily assignable to their places of birth, but it is quite certain that when studied hard enough from that point of view each will be found to have its own definite area of origin. India is at once the occasion and the explanation of the web of Indian thought. But yet, throughout Bengal at any rate, there is a certain definite agreement as to which elements shall be included in the list of yearly celebrations, and in what order. Not all the great things of Indian memory are commemorated thus. There has evidently been a certain selection made and a certain rule imposed by some one or other at some definite time. Throughout Bengal there is no great disagreement as to the festivals and the order in which they occur. The selection must have been made therefore by some person, or body of persons, whose influence was universal in the province. It is a conception that penetrates everywhere, therefore the shaping pressure of this all-pervading influence must have been long-continued. It may have lasted perhaps for centuries. It does not seem to have been a personal influence, for individuals change their policy of government under caprice or circumstance from generation to generation. This would seem rather to have been a steady concensus of opinion, a strong vested interest uniformly exerted in a certain direction. But the complexity of the matter ruled upon, would point to some central seat of counsel and decision again, with as little that was purely personal in its authority as it is possible to imagine. Lastly, whatever was the source of deliberation, it is clear that there must have been a consolidated royal authority to give its support to the decisions of this centre, without flinching or changing, throughout the formative period. Only by a combination of all these conditions can we account for the uniformity and regularity with which so complex a yearly calendar is worked out, from one end of Bengal to the other.

If we wish to be clear about the element of deliberation, let us look, for example, at the Holi festival. In the observance of this day three different factors are distinctly traceable. First, there is a strain of prehistoric Eros-worship, as seen in the villages, in the use of abusive language to women and in the fact that these in their turn are privileged on that day to beat the lords of creation. The conceptions which belong to this phase of the celebration of the full moon of Phalgun must be extremely ancient, and consequently we must look for their analogues and correspondences amongst widely separated branches of the Aryan family, amongst Greek festivals of Love and Spring, for example, in Roman Saturnalia, Mediterranean Carnivals, and even so lately as in the old-fashioned Valentine's Day of English childhood.

That the birth of Chaitanya took place on this very day of Holi Puja, thus determining another of its associations, may seem to some of us an accident. But it was no accident that attempted to interpret the festival in terms of Krishna-worship. Some phase of Hinduism—to which, in the elaborateness of its civilisation, the thought of frank Eros-worship was as revolting and incomprehensible as now to ourselves—some such phase took into its consideration this festival, and decided to reinterpret each of its games and frolics in the light of the gambols of Krishna with the cowherds in the forest of Brindaban. The red powder of the spring-time thus became the blood of the demon Metrasur slain by the Lord. It was natural that the young peasants, under the excitement of danger just escaped, should "blood" one another, and should yearly thereafter burn the effigy of Metrasur in celebration of their deliverance. We can almost hear the voices of those who made the ingenious suggestion!

In the Holi-puja, then, as an instance, we can trace the efforts of some deliberately Hinduising power. This power, it is safe to suppose, is the same that has determined the sacred year as a whole. As a power it must have been ecclesiastical in character, yet must have lived under the *aegis* of a powerful throne. What throne was this? A very simple test is sufficient to answer. Those comparatively modern institutions which are more or less universal to the whole of India, must have derived their original sanction from Pataliputra. Things which are deeply established, and yet peculiar to Bengal, must have emanated from Gour. One of the most important points, therefore, is to determine the geographical distribution of a given observance. In this fact lies the secret of its age.

Historical events as such have never been directly commemorated in India. Yet perhaps, had Guru Govind Singh in the Punjab or Ramdas of Maharashtra lived in the time of the empire of Gour, he would have obtained memorials at the hands of Bengali Hinduism. The fact that none of their age has done so shows that the calendar was complete before their time. Even Chaitanya, born in Bengal itself and a true product of the genius of the people, is scarcely secure in the universal synthesis. His veneration, like that of Buddha, is overmuch confined to those who have surrendered to it altogether. But if in the intellectual sense we would fully understand Chaitanya himself, it is necessary again to study the history of India as a whole, and to realise in what ways he resembled, and in what differed from, other men of his age. What he shared with all India was the great mediæval impulse of Vaishnavism which originated with Ramanuja and swept the country from end to end. That in which his Vaishnavism differed from that of the rest of India represents the characteristic ideas of Bengal under the strong individualising influence of Gour and Vikrampur.

In all that lies around us then, we may, if our eyes are open, read the story of the past. The life we live to-day has been created for us by those who went before us, even as the line of sea-weed on the shore has been placed there by the waves of the tides now over, in their ebb and flow. The present is the wreckage of the past. India as she stands is only to be explained by the history of India. The future waits for us to create it out of the materials left us by the past, aided by our own understanding of this our inheritance.

II

If India itself be the book of Indian history, it follows that travel is the true means of reading that history. The truth of this statement, especially while the published renderings of our history remain so inadequate and so distorted, ought never to be forgotten. Travel as a mode of study is of infinite importance. Yet it is not everything. It is quite possible to travel the world over and see nothing, or only what is not true. We see, after all, only what we are prepared to see. How to develop the mind of the taught so that it shall see, not what its teacher has led it to expect, but the fact that actually passes before the eyes, is the problem of all right scientific education. In history also, we want to be able to see, not the thing that would be pleasant, but the thing that is true. For this we have to go through a strenuous preparation.

With a few of the counters of the game, as it were, we take it for granted that one is already familiar. The great names of Indian history—Buddhism, Saivism, Vaishnavism, Islam—mean something to one. Gradually each student makes for himself his own scale of signs by which to compare the degrees of this or that quality that interests him. He chooses his own episode, and begins to see it in its proper setting. Behar, from its geographical and ethnological position, cannot fail to be one of the most complex and historically interesting provinces in India. In studying Behar, then, we early learn the truth of the dictum of the late Purna Chandra Mukherji, and whenever we find a tamarind, mentally substitute by way of experiment a *bo*-tree; or when we come across a rounded hillock with the grave of a *pir* on the top, convert it into a stupa, and make it a Buddhist centre.[1] If we do this and cultivate the habit of

[1] To the Mohammedan the tamarind tree is holy, and the fact that on entering Behar he would plant it in the place of the *bo*, or take the trouble to build a *pir's* tomb on a rounded hillock, goes far to show that the sacred character of the tree and hill was still at that moment maintained in Behar. That is to say, Buddhism was remembered.

summing up our impressions, we shall be led to many wonderful and unexpected conclusions about the distribution of population at the Mohammedan invasion, the strength and forms of Buddhism, and so on.

But one of the master-facts in Indian history, a fact borne in upon us more deeply with every hour of study, is that India is and always has been a synthesis. No amount of analysis—racial, lingual, or territorial—will ever amount in the sum to the study of India. Perhaps the axioms of Euclid are not axioms after all. Perhaps all the parts of a whole are not equal to the whole. At any rate, apart from and above all the fragments which must be added together to make India, we have to recognise India herself, all-containing, all-dominating, moulding and shaping the destinies and the very nature of the elements out of which she is composed. The Indian people may be defective in the methods of mechanical organisation, but they have been lacking, as a people, in none of the essentials of organic synthesis. No Indian province has lived unto itself, pursuing its own development, following its own path, going its way unchallenged and alone. On the contrary, the same tides have swept the land from end to end. A single impulse has bound province to province at the same period, in architecture, in religion, in ethical striving. The provincial life has been rich and individual, yet over and above it all India has known how to constitute herself a unity, consciously possessed of common hopes and common loves. Thus in the pursuit of epochs and parts we must never forget the Motherland behind them all. In remembering her and turning to her, again and again we shall find the explanation that had baffled us, discover the link that we required.

We must not be cowed too easily by proofs that such and such a cherished idea had a foreign or semi-foreign origin. In this world there is no such thing as real originality. Some mind more powerful than others breaks up common symbols into their elements and recombines these in an unexpected fashion. This is the whole of what we call originality. The proof of a mind's vigour lies in its ability to work upon the materials it meets with. What is true of persons is true in this respect of nations. Some achievements, because we do not know their history, appear unique, solitary, miraculous. In reality civilisations like religions are a web; they are not statues or *salon*-pictures, great creations of individual genius. If we could unveil the spectacle of the genesis of Greece, we should find links between common and uncommon in every department of her extraordinary output, and much that now seems unaccountable for its beauty or its boldness would then appear inevitable. The fact that Egypt, Assyria, and the East itself were all within hail, had more to do with the peculiar form taken by the Greek genius than we are now prepared to grant. If so, the actual glory of Hellenic culture lay in the distinctiveness of its touch, and the energy of its manipulation, of the materials that came its way. Perhaps above even these qualities was a certain faculty of discrimination and organisation in which it excelled. But in any case the Greek race would not have produced the Greek civilisation in any other geographical or ethnological position than the one which they happened to occupy. The utmost that can be said in praise of any special people is that they have known how to give a strong impress of their own to those materials which the world of their time brought to their door. If this be the high-water mark then of national achievement, what is there to be said for that of India? Has she, or has she not, a touch of her own that is unmistakable? Surely it was a knowledge of the answer that led us to this question. Even in decorative matters the thing that is Indian cannot be mistaken for the product of any other nationality. Who can fail to recognise the Indian, the Assyrian, the Egyptian, or the Chinese touch in, for example, the conventionalising of a lotus? In form, in costume, in character, and above all, in thought, the thing that is Indian is unlike any un-Indian thing in the whole world. For the mind that tends to be depressed by the constant talk of Indian debts to foreign sources, the best medicine is a few minutes' quiet thought as to what India has done with it all. Take refuge for a moment in the Indian world that you see around you. Think of your history. Is it claimed that some other people made Buddhism?

Or that Shiva with his infinite renunciation was a dream of Europe? No: if India shared a certain fund of culture elements with other peoples, that is nothing to be unhappy about. The question is not, where did they come from? but what has she made out of them? Has India been equal to her opportunities at every period? Has she been strong enough to take all that she knew to be in the world at each given period, and assimilate it, and nationalise it in manner and use? No one in his senses would deny this of India. Therefore she has nothing of shame or mortification to fear from any inquiry into culture origins.

This nightmare being disposed of, there is still another. The Indian mind can hardly help making questions of antiquity into partisan arguments. Perhaps this is natural; but in any case it is a great barrier to the popularising of real historical inquiry. The mind of the student ought to be absolutely open on the point of dates. If there is the least bias in favour of one direction or the other, it is just like a weight on one side of a balance. Fair measure does not come that way! As a matter of fact, the strictly historical period in India may be comparatively short, something less than thirty centuries, but there can be no difference of opinion as to the vast length of the total period of evolution. The oldest problems of the world's history have their field of study here. Those sociological inquiries that lie behind all history must be pursued in India. History proper only emerges when a certain group of people becomes sufficiently consolidated to carry on common activities in a direction and with a motive that we may call political. Man as the political animal is the subject of history. This is a stage that will be arrived at soonest by communities which are relatively small and compact, and inhabit clearly defined geographical confines, on the frontiers of other populations not greatly unlike themselves in civilisation. Thus Egypt, Nineveh, and Babylon could not but arrive sooner than India on the historical stage in virtue of their very nearness to one another. But this does not necessarily mean that they could compete with her in actual age, or in the depth of the tendencies making for their evolution. And in any case, while these are dead, India lives and develops still, responds still to all the living influences of the world about her, and sees before her, as the individual unit that her development has made her, a long vista of growth and perfection to be achieved. The art and architecture of Egypt date from four thousand years before the Christian era. Crete had a story almost as early. Who shall say what was the age of Babylon? But we must remember that when all these were already mature, India was still a-making. A long childhood, say the biologists, is the greatest proof of evolutionary advancement. Egypt, with her exceptional climate, made art and architecture the supreme expression of her national existence. India put her powers, perhaps as long ago, into the dreams and philosophy of the Upanishads. Cities would have crumbled into dust, temples and carvings would have succumbed in a few aeons to the ravages of time. Human thought, written on the least permanent and most ephemeral of all materials, is nevertheless the most enduring of all the proofs of our antiquity. Who shall say that we have not chosen the better part? Every generation destroys the parchment of our record, and yet a million generations only make its truth the more assured. We can hardly dig so deep into the past as to come upon the time when in Egypt, or Greece, or Crete, or Babylon, the name of India had not already a definite sound and association. At the very dawn of history in Europe, her thought and scholarship were already held in that respect which is akin to awe. His old tutor in the fourth century before Christ begs Alexander to bring him an Indian scholar! There is no need for discontent in the Indian mind, if those activities of which the historic muse can take account, activities intertribal, international, political, began for her comparatively late. India, alone of all the nations of antiquity, is still young, still growing, still keeping a firm hold upon her past, still reverently striving of it to weave her future. Are not these things enough for any single people?

At the same time, when these conditions are loyally recognised and accepted, we cannot doubt that the result will be a continual snatching of new morsels out of the night of the prehistoric to be brought within the lighted circle of history. This will happen still more constantly if students try to saturate themselves with the social habit of thought, that is to say, if they will accustom themselves to thinking of the human and psychological facts behind events. Only this habit can teach them when to postulate tribes and peoples for the individual names in ancient ballads, or when to read a war of migration and conquest for a battle. Only this can give them a sense of scale with which to measure the drift and tendency of the forces coming into play during certain epochs. To multiply here and divide there is very necessary, yet is only to be done rightly by one who is accustomed to think sociologically.

The sociological habit is essential also if we would be in a position to gauge the relations of India to the incomers from beyond her border. Few people know that in the beginnings of human society woman was the head of the family, and not man. Queens, who seem to us now something of an anomaly, represent an institution older than that of kings. In certain nations the memory of this ancient time of mother-rule is still deeply ingrained. Others, like the Aryans, have long ago passed out of it. And some fragmentary communities in the world remain still more or less on the border line between the two. Only a deep familiarity with the traces of these different phases can give us a real clue to the history of Asia. Only a grasp of that history will enable us to compute distances of time truly. How old a given institution is it may be impossible to say in terms of years, but we can tell at a glance whether it is matriarchal or patriarchal, or by what combination of two societies it may have arisen. The thought of goddesses is older than that of gods, just as the idea of queens is prior to that of kings.

The history of common things and their influence on our customs is a study that follows naturally on that of human society. Much of this we can make out for ourselves. For instance, we can see that the ass must be older than the horse as a beast of burden. Once upon a time the world had no steeds, no carrier, save this useful if humble servant of man. Let us dream for a while of this. Let us study the present distribution of the donkey, and find out his name in various Aryan languages. All that the horse now is, as a figure in poetry, the ass must once have been. Noblest, fleetest, bravest and nearest to man of all the four-footed kind, men would set no limit to their admiration for him. The Goddess Sitola rides upon a donkey, because, in that dim past out of which she comes, there were as yet no horses tamed by man. There was once no steed so royal as the milk-white ass, which is now relegated here to the use of *dhobies*, while numerous are the allusions to its use, and the glory thereof, in the older Jewish scriptures. The very fact that it appears in the account of the Royal Entrance, in the Christian story, points to the old association of splendour clinging longer to the name of the ass in Arab countries than elsewhere, and in harmony with this is the fact that it is widely distributed throughout Africa. After the horse was once tamed, men would never have taken the trouble necessary to reclaim the ass, and from this alone we may judge of its great antiquity. At the same time we may form an idea of the time and effort spent on the gradual domestication of wild animals, when we read the reiterated modern opinion that the zebra cannot be tamed. Primitive man would not so easily have given up the struggle. But then he would not either have expected so quick and profitable a result. In the story of the commonest things that lie about us we may, aided by the social imagination, trace out the tale of the far past.

Thus the mind comes to live in the historic atmosphere. It becomes ready to learn for itself from what it sees about it at home and on a journey. The search for stern truth is the best fruit of the best scientific training. But the truth is not necessarily melancholy, and Indian students will do most to help the growth of knowledge if they begin with the robust conviction that in the long tale of their Motherland there can be nothing to cause them anything but pride and reverence. What is truly interpreted cannot but redound to the vindication and encouragement of India and the Indian people.

THE CITIES OF BUDDHISM

ACCEPTING the theory that Buddhism was developed in India, not as a sect or church, but only as a religious order, founded by one of the greatest of the World-Teachers, we find ourselves compelled to account for the relations that would arise between the king or the populace impressed by the memory of Buddha, and the order that followed in his succession and bore his name.

To do this, however, it is first necessary that we should have some determinate idea as to where, in the India of the Buddhist period, were the great centres of population. An Indian city, it has been well said, is a perishable thing, and it is easy to think of names which would justify the statement. No one who has seen the Dhauli Rock, for instance, seven miles away from Bhubaneshwar, can imagine that the edict it bears, fronted by the royal cognisance of the elephant head, was originally sculptured in the wild woods where it now stands. A glance is enough to tell us that the circular ditch which surrounds the fields below was once the moat of a city, backed and fortified by the Dhauli Hill itself, and that the edict-bearing rock stood at the south-eastern corner of this city, where the high-road from the coast must have reached and entered the gates. This city of Dhauli was the capital, doubtless, of Kalinga, when Asoka in his military youth conquered the province. In order to estimate its value and importance in the age to which it belonged, we must first restore to the mind's eye the ports of Tamralipti and Puri, deciding which of these two was the Liverpool of the Asokan era. A theocratic institution such as pilgrimage is frequently a sort of precipitate from an old political condition, and almost always embodies elements of one sort or another which have grown up in a preceding age. Presumably, therefore, Puri was the great maritime centre of the pre-Christian centuries in Northern India; and if so, a road must have passed from it, through Dhauli, to Pataliputra in the north. By this road went and came the foreign trade between India and the East, and between the north and south. In the age of the Kesari kings of Orissa, not only had Dhauli itself given place to Bhubaneshwar, but Puri, perhaps by the same process, had been superseded by Tamralipti, the present Tamluk. It was at the second of these that Fa Hian in the fifth century embarked on his return voyage. Such a supersession of one port by another, however, would only be completed very gradually, and for it to happen at all we should imagine that there must have been a road from one to the other along the coast. If only the covering sands could now be excavated along that line, there is no saying what discoveries might be made of buried temples and transitional cities. For a whole millennium in history would thus be brought to light.

On the great road from Dhauli to the north, again, there must have been some point at which a route branched off for Benares, passing through Gaya, and crossing the Punpun River, following in great part the same line by which Shere Shah's *dâk* went later and the railway goes to-day.

Let us suppose, however, that two thousand and more years have rolled away, and that we are back once more in that era in which Dhauli was a fortified capital city. The elephant-heralded decree stands outside the gates, proclaiming in freshly-cut letters of the common tongue the name of that wise and just Emperor who binds himself and his people by a single body of law.

"I, King Piyadassi, in the twelfth year after my anointing, have obtained true enlightenment," the august edict begins. It goes on to express the royal distress at the imperialistic conquest of the province, in Asoka's youth, and assures his people of his desire to mitigate this fundamental injustice of his rule by a readiness to give audience to any one of them, high or low, at any hour of the day or night. It further enumerates certain of the departments of public works which have been established by the new government, such as those of wells, roads, trees, and medicine. And it notes the appointment of public censors, or guardians of morality.

In his reference to the obtaining of "true enlightenment" Asoka records himself a non-monastic disciple of the great monastic order of the day. Nearly three hundred years have elapsed since the passing of the Blessed One, and in the history of the Begging Friars whom He inaugurated there has been heretofore no event like this, of the receiving of the imperial penitent into the lay-ranks served by them. Their task of nation-making is slowly but surely going forward nevertheless. In the light of the Gospel of Nirvana the Aryan Faith is steadily defining and consolidating itself. The Vedic gods have dropped out of common reference. The religious ideas of the Upanishads are being democratised by the very labours of the Begging Friars in spreading those of Buddha, and are coming to be regarded popularly as a recognised body of doctrine characteristic of the Aryan folk. Vague racial superstitions about snakes and trees and sacred springs are tending more and more to be intellectually organised and regimented round the central figure of Brahma, the creator and ordainer of Brahmanic thinkers.

Thus the higher philosophical conceptions of the higher race are being asserted as the outstanding peaks and summits of the Hinduistic faith, and the current notions of the populace are finding their place gradually in the body of that faith, coming by degrees into organic continuity with the lofty abstractions of the Upanishads. In other words, the making of Hinduism has begun.

The whole is fermented and energised by the memory of the Great Life, ended only three centuries agone, of which the yellow-clad brethren are earnest and token. Had Buddha founded a church, recognising social rites, receiving the new-born, solemnising marriage, and giving benediction to the passing soul, his personal teachings would have formed to this hour a distinguishable half-antagonistic strain in the organ-music of Hinduism. But he founded only an order. And its only function was to preach the Gospel and give individual souls the message of Nirvana. For marriage and blessing, men must go to the Brahmans: the sons of Buddha could not be maintainers of the social polity, since in his eyes it had been the social nexus itself which had constituted that World, that *Maya*, from which it was the mission of the Truth to set men free.

The work of the monk, then, as a witness to the eternal verities, was in no rivalry to the more civic function of the Brahmanic priesthood. And this is the fact which finds expression in the relation of the monkhood to the Indian cities of the Asokan era. The Brahman is a citizen-priest, living in a city. The Buddhist is a monk, living in an abbey. In all lands the monk has memorialised himself by buildings instead of by posterity. In India these have been largely carved, as at

Mahavellipore in the south, or excavated, as at Ellora and elsewhere, instead of built. But the sentiment is the same. In place of a single monastery with its chapel or cathedral, we find here a number of independent cells or groups of cells, and frequently a whole series of cathedral shrines. Apparently a given spot has remained a monastic centre during generation after generation. Dynasties and revolutions might come and go, but this would remain, untouched by any circumstance save the inevitable shifting of population and the final decay of its own spiritual fire.

In its decoration the abbey would reflect the art of the current epoch. In culture it would act as a university. In ideals it represented the super-social, or extra-civic conception of the spiritual equality and fraternity of all men. Its inmates were vowed to religious celibacy. And we may take it that *the place of the abbey would always be at a certain distance from a city whose government was in sympathy with it.*

Thus the city of Dhauli, under the Emperor Asoka and succeeding worshippers of Buddha, had Khandagiri at seven miles' distance as its royal abbey. The civic power was represented at Gaya: the monastic at Bodh-Gaya. Benares was the seat of Brahmans: Sarnath of monks. Elephanta was the cathedral-temple of a king's capital,[1] but Kenheri, on another island a few miles away, offers to us the corresponding monastery.

[1] And Elephanta is of considerably later date.

From these examples and from what we can see to have been their inevitableness, we might expect that any important city of the Buddhistic period would be likely to occur in connection with a monastic centre some few miles distant. Now it is possible to determine the positions of a great many such cities on grounds entirely *a priori.* It is clear, for instance, that whatever geographical considerations might make Benares great would also act at the same time to distinguish Allahabad. By a similar induction, Mathura on the Jumna and Hardwar on the Ganges might also be expected to furnish proof of ancient greatness. Now outside Prayag we have to the present time, as a haunt of *sadhus,* the spot known as Nirvanikal. And in the vicinity of Hardwar, is there not Hrishikesh? The caves of Ellora have near them the town of Roza. But this we must regard as a sort of Mohammedan priory, inasmuch as its population consists mainly of religious beggars (of course not celibate) living about the tomb of Aurangzebe. The neighbouring capital that supported the youth of Ellora was probably at Deogiri, now called Daulatabad.

It is the broken links in the chain, however, that fascinate us most in the light of this historical generalisation. What was the city, and what the state, that made Ajanta possible? What was the city that corresponded to the *dharmsala* at Sanchi? What was the city, and what the abbey, in the case of Amravati?

Undoubtedly a fashion once started in such strength under Buddha-worshipping sovereigns and commonwealths would tend to be imitated in later ages when the system of ideas that we know as Hinduism had come more definitely into vogue. It is also possible that when the Buddhistic orders failed or died out their places were sometimes taken, in the ancient *maths* and foundations, by Jain religious. Something of this sort appears at least to have happened at Sarnath and possibly at Khandagiri also. But the whole history of the relations between Brahmans, Buddhists, and Jains wants working out from an Asiatic and not European point of view, if many pages of history are to become clear to us.

One question of great interest that arises in this connection, is, What of this parallelism in the case of Pataliputra? Going back to Rajgir, we see the early ancestral capital of the Nanda kings confronted, at least in later ages, by Nalanda, the historic university of Bengal, to which Hiouen Tsang owed so much. But what of Pataliputra itself? Can we suppose that the imperial seat had no official *ashrama* of piety and learning in its vicinity? Yet if it had, and if perhaps the "Five Pahars" mark the site of this religious college, what was the situation of the capital in regard to it?

Again we find place and occasion, by means of this generalisation, for more definite consideration than was hitherto possible of Indian culture and civilisation at various epochs. What were the various functions performed by these great extra-civic priories? No Englishman has reason to be prouder of Oxford than the Hindu of Ajanta. The eternal antithesis of Europe between "town and gown" was never a source of rioting and disorder in the East, only because from the beginning they were recognised by universal consent as distinct entities, whose separateness of interests demanded a certain geographical distance. What was the life lived in these royal abbeys, whose foundations date back in so many cases—notably Bodh-Gaya, Sarnath, Dhauli, and Sanchi—even earlier than the reign of Asoka himself? They were a symbol of democracy to the eyes of the whole community, of the right of every man to the highest spiritual career. It is not conceivable that they should have been entirely without influence on the education of youth. But undoubtedly their main value intellectually lay in their character of what we should now call post-graduate universities.

Here must have been carried on such researches as were recorded, in the lapse of centuries, by Patanjali, in his *Yoga Aphorisms*, one of the most extraordinary documents of ancient science known to the world. Here must have been the home of that learning which made the golden age of the Guptas possible, between 300 and 500 A.D. We must think too of the international relations of these ancient monastic colleges. Fa Hian (400 A.D.) and Hiouen Tsang (650 A.D.) were not the only eastern students who came in the ages that followed the Christian era to drink of the springs of Indian learning. They were a couple whose books of travels happen to have become famous. But they were two out of a great procession of pilgrim-scholars. And it was to the abbeys that such came. It was from these abbeys, again, that the missions proceeded to foreign countries. No nation was ever evangelised by a single teacher. The word *Patrick* in Irish, it is said, means *praying-man*, and the vaunted saint is thus, beyond a doubt, either a member or a personification of a whole race of Christian preachers who carried Baptism and the Cross to early Ireland. Similarly Mahinda, Nagarjuna, and Bodhidharmma in the twelfth century, were not the isolated figures painted by history as we know it. They were merely conspicuous elements in a whole stream of missionary effort, that radiated from the quiet abbeys and monasteries of India in its great ages towards the worlds of east and west. Christianity itself, it has been often suggested, may have been one of the later fruits of such a mission, as preached in Persia and Syria.

Here, in these lovely retreats—for they are all placed in the midst of natural beauty—was elaborated the thought and learning, the power of quiet contemplation, and the marvellous energy of art and literary tradition, that have made India as we know her to-day. Here were dreamed those dreams which, reflected in society, became the social ideals of the ages in which we live. And here was demonstrated the great law that will be expressed again and again in history, whenever the glory of India rises to one of its supreme moments, the law of the antithesis between city and university, between *samaj* and religious orders, between the life of affairs and the life of thought. Antithetic as they are, however, these are nevertheless complementary. Spirituality brings glory in its train. The monastic life reacts to make civic strength.

RAJGIR: AN ANCIENT BABYLON

Up, up, up. The long array of steps seems endless, as we climb the steep hillside to reach the dwelling that has been lent us for a few weeks' habitation; and, after all, when we come upon it, it is nothing but a nest of robber-barons, this old manor-house of the Rajas of Annwa. A nest of robber-barons, truly, perched half-way up the mountain and concealed from sight, and yet with a wide stretch of country well in its own purview. Curiously small and unfortified to Western thinking, it consists of two parts—a court on the inside guarded against intrusion and crowned with wide terrace-roofs; and without, a few rooms ranged about two sides of an open square. Its feudal and mediæval character lends the building an interest which its undeniable beauty well sustains. But far beyond either of these considerations is the exciting fact that we are to keep house for twenty-one days in a spot where for a period of from twenty-five to thirty centuries there has been continuously a human habitation. For the great staircase by which we have climbed the rugged hillside is undoubtedly constructed over the foundations of the ancient walls of Rajgir, and the earliest predecessor of the Barons of Annwa must have chosen for his family stronghold to develop one of the buttresses of the guardroom of the selfsame walls, occurring on a small plateau. Below us lies the floor of the winding pass with the stream that forms a moat at the foot of our mountain-stairway. In front a great curving staircase, constituting what our modern railway companies would call a loop of the fort, protects those temples and hot springs of Rajgir which still form the objective of a yearly Hindu pilgrimage. And out in the open, a stone's throw away as it seems in this clear plain atmosphere, but really perhaps a mile by the road, is the modern village of Rajgir, anciently Ràja-Griha, the city or dwelling-place of kings.

Already the villagers are showing us friendly attentions. The servant who has come with us was born a few miles away, and his womenfolk are arriving with our first meal in hospitable readiness. The peasant-guard have established themselves in the outer rooms for our protection, and a small boy of the neighbourhood is clamouring to be taken on as an attendant. It is as if we were guests of Semiramis in Nineveh of old! It is like pitching our tent on the ruins of Babylon, and entering into friendly relations with lineal descendants of the ancient inhabitants!

How beautiful is the country that lies stretched before us! Outward from the mouth of our twisting pass, at Christmas time or thereabouts, it will be covered in the green of rice and other crops, with every here and there a field of white opium-poppies in full bloom. But now, at the change of the season in October, we see here fields as patches of many-coloured earth—purple and brown and red—and we remember the words of Buddha, half laughing doubtless yet full of affectionate memory and tenderness, of one who said to a disciple in a much-patched garment that he reminded him of the ricefields about Rajgir.

A quarter of a mile behind us the hills open out into a circle, and here lie the ruins of the ancient city of kings—wonderfully clear and distinct in every part of them. We almost might trace out the very lines of the bazaars. With regard to streets and roads, it sounds dangerously near truism to say that they retain their positions with little change from age to age, yet I do not know that the fact has been much noted. Here in Rajgir at any rate, where hundreds of cows and buffaloes, sheep and goats, are driven daily by the herds to and from the ancient ruins, many of the main roadways remain much as they must have been in the dim past. Here, for instance, is the thoroughfare that ran through the city, with traces at a certain point near the centre of the palace walls, bastions, and gateways; and here beyond the palace are the outlines of the royal pleasure-grounds, with their wonderfully engineered ornamental waters intact to this day. All through this little mountain-arena and the pass that leads to it, indeed, there has been an extraordinary amount of hydraulic engineering. It would seem as if the fame of the hot springs must have been the original cause of the royal settlement in this natural fortress, and the artificial development of its streams the main occupation of the kingly line thereafter. Even now below our own walled and moated manor lies an empty tank that two thousand years ago most likely held lotuses in a park. Even now the river that runs through the valley, though naturally one, is divided in parts into two and even three streams, forming a network that is enough to show us the attention that must have been paid in ancient India to the problems of irrigation, in order to give birth to so marvellous a degree of hydraulic science. Far away in Central India is a monumental building, of an age some two hundred years later than that of Old Rajgir, which shows by its ornamental cascades the same engineering genius, and the same royal idea of beauty and magnificence as we find here. Well may the Indian people glory in the ancestry which already lived in this splendour, while that of Northern and Western Europe went clad in painted woad.

There can be a few places in the world so old as Rajgir, about which so much is definitely known and so much safely to be inferred. It was in all probability about the year 590 B.C.—in a world in which Babylon and Phœnicia and Egypt and Sheba were of all facts most living and important —it was about the year 590 B.C. that there came along the road leading into the valley yonder, one

BUDDHA AND THE LAME KID.

From Water-colour by Nanda Lal Bose.

whose very form was radiant with feeling and thought, that lifted him above the common world into that consciousness that makes history.

It may have been early morning when He came. For the books say that the great company of goats was being led up at that moment for the royal sacrifice; fixed, it may have been, for about the hour of noon. Or it may have been about the time of cowdust, on the eve of the festival, and the herdsmen may have intended to stable their goats for that night outside the palace. In any case He came, some say carrying on his shoulder a lame kid, followed by the patter of thousands of little hoofs. He came, moreover, in a passion of pity. A veritable storm of compassion had broken loose within him on behalf of these, the helpless "little brothers" of humanity, who were caught like man himself in the net of pain and pleasure, of life and death; bewildered like man by love and sorrow, but who unlike man for want of speech could neither express their perplexity nor form a conception of release. Surely they crowded round Him, and rubbed themselves against Him again and again, the gentle, wondering, four-footed things! For the animals are strangely susceptible to the influence of a silent love that has no designs on their life or freedom. All the legends of the world tell us that they catch the hush of Christmas Eve, respond to the eager questioning of the Child Dhruva, and understand that unmeasured yearning to protect them which may be read in the eyes of the Lord Buddha on the road that goes up to the palace of Rajgir.

We had been some time in the place before we noticed that it was on one particular islet in the river below us that the village deathfires might so often be seen at evening. It was a very ancient custom in India to burn the dead by the stream-side just outside the town. But this sandbank was far away from the village. Hardly could they have chosen a point less easily accessible. Ah, yes! certainly there was the explanation; the burning *ghât* of these peasants in the twentieth century must be still where their ancestors had chosen it, in the fifth, in the first—aye, even for centuries before that—maybe immediately without the city of Old Rajgir. It takes a peculiar angle of vision, and perhaps a peculiar mood of passivity, to see the trees turn into a forest when the existence of such was previously unsuspected. So I shall not attempt to guess how many more evenings elapsed before, as we went along the roadway on the far side of the burning *ghât*, one of us noted the broken steps and the entwined tamarind and *bo*-trees that marked the old-time *ghât* of Rajgir. Nor do I know how many more days went by before there came to some one of us the flash of insight that led us finally to discover that the mass of fallen masonry close by was that very ancient gateway of the city through which Buddha himself with the goats must have passed, and brought to our notice the dome-like head of an old stupa lying in the dust a few feet away.

Passing through the gate and standing at the opening of the theatre-like valley, we find that the river which flows out of the city as one, is made up of two streams which between them encircle the royal city as a moat, even within its girdle of mountains and its enclosing walls. They join at this point. Leaving unexplored that which flows towards us from the left part of the garden of Ambapali, the Indian Mary Magdalene, and past the abodes of many of the characters who figure in the narrative of Buddha's life, we may turn to that branch which comes to us from the right.

A world of discoveries awaits us here! The path leads us across to the water, but this is easily forded by stepping-stones which may still be detected as fragments of an ancient bathing *ghât*. Evidently bathing and the bathing-*ghât* were as prominent in the Indian civilisation twenty-five centuries ago as they are to-day. Then the road follows the streamside at a distance of some fifty yards more or less from the line of mountains on the right. About midway through the city the face of this mountain is pierced by a great cave, known to-day to the peasants of the countryside as the Sonar Bhandar or Golden Treasury. The interior of this cave is polished, not carved. There stands in it, as if some party of robbers had been interrupted in an attempt to carry it away, the earliest stupa I have ever seen. The outside is half concealed by shrubs and creepers. But even now the mortice-holes remain that show where the carved wooden ornaments were once attached. And even now as we stand at the entrance we see in the distance, in the middle of the city, the tower that Fa Hian noted as still intact and visible in the year A.D. 404, crowning a small stupa or well to the east of the palace.

This cave then was the cathedral of Old Rajgir. Here Buddha must have rested or meditated or taught; and there must, suggested some member of our party, have been a roadway connecting it directly with the palace. Acting on this clue, we proceeded to brush aside the wild growths and explore the line between the two. Outside the cave we found a level floor of ancient asphalt, a sort of Venetian Plaza de San Marco as it were. This was evidently the town square. We read a reference in one of the old Chinese *suttas* of a certain place in Rajgir—as the place where the peacocks were fed. "The place where the peacocks were fed"; how our minds had lingered over the words when we first read them! And now here we stand. For undoubtedly just as the pigeons are fed outside St. Paul's, so on this asphalt plaza, before the cathedral entrance in an Eastern city, it fitted the royal dignity and bounty that peacocks should be daily given grain.

The asphalt runs down to the river and across it. For the water still flows under the ancient bridge, and we can walk on it though its level is somewhat sunken. Easily, then, we make our way to the royal mansion, clearly marked as this is at its four corners by the foundations of four bastion towers. But turning again to the bridge, we find an unbroken line of this same asphalt running along the bank by the way we have come, though sooth to say we might never have noticed it if we had not been tracing it out from the conspicuous mass.

Was this, the river-front opposite to the palace, protected by the steep hills behind, and running from the town plaza to the bathing *ghât* beyond, and across this to the city gates—was this the High Street of the ancient town? Every now and again, as day after day we pace brooding up and down the distance, every now and again we come upon some hitherto unnoticed mass of masonry or mason's tool-marks. Here are a couple of blocks lying on their sides, as if to form a seat in a river-wall. Here again traces of steps or fallen ornaments. At one place on the opposite bank, deeply sunk between masses of earth and vegetation, there runs down to the riverside a small ravine that would now pass as a gully if the pavement or ancient asphalt did not prove it—in days before Pompeii and Herculaneum were born—to have been a street.

What were the houses like that looked down upon these footways? What was the life that was lived in them? How long had the place been a city? How long did it continue to be one? What were the surroundings in the height of its glory of this abode of kings, now an austere and desolate ruin? These and a thousand other questions crowd upon us, and it is strange to how many of them we can give an answer. The rushing rains of Indian summers have long washed away most of the soil from the hanging gardens that once clothed the hillsides, and made the prospect from the palace to the gates and beyond them through the pass leading out into the plains a veritable vision of delight.

But still the artificial terraces of red trap-rock are smooth and level amidst the out-cropping masses of natural crags, and still the wanderer may take his stand on some spot whence Bimbisara the king was wont to look upon the glories of his inheritance, or, with difficulty at one or two points, may trace the way through the old pleasance by which doubtless royal hunting-parties may have started for the forest-glades. To-day, it is true, there are no rich woodlands covering slopes and mountain-tops, as in the royal ages. Wild undergrowth, dense shrubs, and here and there a twisted palm growing in a cranny are all that can stand for the lofty timbers, dense aisles of the days when the place was a paradise, a king's garden surrounding a king's palace. And still at the back of the ruined city, guarding it from the passes on the south and east, we find the double walls of enormous thickness.

The square mortice-holes in the face of the rock out of which the great Sonar Bhandar is hollowed, give us a clue that enables us to rebuild, mentally, the ancient city. For these mortice-holes held the attachments of the wooden ornaments that formed the front of the cave. Now, between Bombay and Poona, on the west of India, is another cave, that of Karli, which though of a much later date must be of the same style and period as this, and there the wooden front is still intact. Moreover, the carvings form a picture, as Fergusson has pointed out, of an ancient street, from which we gather that the second storeys of houses standing in rows were decorated in front with crowded wooden verandahs, porches, niches, and all sorts of beautiful and irregular curved corners. That these, further, were not mere devices of beauty in the case of the houses, as they were in those of the caves, we see in the pictures which were carved, probably in the first or second century A.D., on the gateways of Sanchi. From these we can gather an idea of what the palace of Bimbisara and the homes of his subjects must have been like. The first storey, then, was massive, sloping inwards and upwards, loopholed and buttressed at its four corners by four circular towers. The first storey only was built of stone, and its parapet was battlemented. On the strong terrace provided by the roof of this fortification were constructed the family living rooms, which were of wood and much carved. That it would have been possible, however, to withdraw the women into the lower storey in time of war may be seen from buried ruins at Ujjain, which are shown by the *pandas* as part of Vikramaditya's palace, and appear to have belonged to a fortress of Asoka's time. Here, built of hard grey stone now black with age we have what seems to be the inside corner, and part of the courtyard, of just such a building as the Sanchi sculptures would lead us to expect as the dwelling of a king or noble. Outside, the walls would be almost blind; inside, they are honeycombed with many-pillared halls and verandahs, and one room with raised floor that represents an old Indian form of bedchamber and bed in one. In times of peace these were, we may suppose, the quarters assigned to men-at-arms. The building is of a massiveness that rivals nature, and there are a few pillars still left—amongst the many that the succeeding sovereigns decorated in different degrees and different styles—whose simplicity of form enables any observer that knows Sanchi to feel fairly confident in assigning the building as a whole to the reign of Asoka, or earlier.

Of such a form, then, though perhaps smaller and less elaborate, may we suppose the palace of Rajgir to have been, and in the streets about it the more plebeian dwellings of the townsfolk must, though small and comparatively huddled, have been like unto it. True, their lower storeys would be built, in all probability, even as the huts of the Rajgir pilgrims are to this day, of mud and pebbles, instead of lordly stone. From hillocks formed of such deposits, anyone may pick out by the streamside, at various different levels, bits of old household pottery. But the facings and tops of the shops and houses were doubtless of carved wood, and the front of the cathedral was a faithful enough reflex of the life of the town. Through such streets, while the king stood watching him from the roof of the palace, paced the Sakya Prince, "a lad in his first youth," ere yet he was Buddha, and no honour that Bimbisara could offer would tempt him from that bridal of Poverty in which alone his mind delighted. "This life of the household is pain, free only is he who lives in the open air"; thinking thus he embraced the life of the wandering monk.

Far away from Rajgir, in the north of Rajputana, we have Amber and Jaipur, a couple of cities which every visitor to India tries to see. Of these, Amber is situated in the highlands, and Jaipur out in the plain, Amber being, of course, very much the older of the two. It is in fact an old Indian doctrine that no city should occupy the same ground for more than a thousand years. It is supposed that a potent means of avoiding pestilence and other ills is then to move out and occupy a new space. In accordance with this canon the new city of Jaipur was laid out. And when all was finished, the Maharaja moved into the new town with all his people.

Now this history of Amber and Jaipur, enacted in modern India and still fresh in the memory of the Rajput people, is our guide to much in the history of Old Rajgir. For in the lifetime of Buddha, the son of Bimbisara—that tragic king, Ajatasatru, across whose path falls the red shadow of a father's murder !—found that the time had come to move the city of kings, and he accordingly built a new city with walls and gates like the last but out in the open plain. And there the grass-covered ruin lies to this day, to the west of the present village, the grave of a city, the memorial of New Rajgir.

Bimbisara was the king of Magadha in the days of the Great Renunciation. Ajatasatru was king at the death of Buddha. But we know, from the fact of the desertion of their highland stronghold and its rebuilding outside, that for five hundred years at least before their time there had been a city on the site of Old Rajgir.

Nor need we think that the city thus built was only a palace and its appurtenances. The fact that it actually became the new centre of population, forming the direct ancestor of the present village, shows itself two hundred years later, when the great Asoka, desiring to build fitting memorials to Him whom the emperor delighted to honour, chose its north-western corner, on the left hand of the main gateway, whereat to place a stupa and Asokan pillar with an inscription. As the edicts carved by Asoka on rocks and pillars have the character of proclamations, it follows that the rocks and pillars themselves partake somewhat of the nature of the modern journal, inasmuch as they were the means adopted to publish the royal will, and hence a position could never be selected for them at a distance from inhabited cities. The inscribed pillar at Sarnath was placed at the door or in the courtyard of a monastery. And similarly the inscribed pillars, whose fragments have been found at Pataliputra, were erected in the interior or on the site of the old jail as an act of imperial penance.

We may take it, then, that Old Rajgir was really deserted at about the time of Bimbisara's successor, and, if it was afterwards used as a royal residence, was so used at intervals, as Amber is now. Such then was the city, already ancient, through which Buddha himself has passed time and again and where He was held by all as an honourable guest. Across these fields and up and down these streets, now ruined, or within the massive cathedral-cave of Sonar Bhandar, there echo to this hour the immortal reverberations of Buddha's voice.

Why did He come this way at all? Was it for the sake of the learned men who forgather in the neighbourhood of capitals? Was the famous university of Nalanda of after-ages already perhaps a university, where one might come in the sure hope of finding all the wisdom of the age? It would seem as if, any way, He passed this spot with treasure already in the heart, needing only long years of brooding thought to fuse his whole Self in its realisation. Unless he was sure of the truth before He reached here, He could not have gone, sure and straight as an arrow from the bow, to the unfrequented forest of bel-trees, with its cave overhanging the river, and its great tree between the farms and ponds, where now the humble village of Bodh-Gaya stands.

BEHAR

FROM Patna on the east to Benares on the west, stretch in the month of January fields of white poppies all abloom. In this Holy Land of the Buddhist nations blossoms to-day this flower of death. The earth where it grows was made sacred long ago by the feet of Buddha. At the site of the ancient Pataliputra, almost where Bankipore stands to-day, He entered the kingdom of Magadha. For ages they called the river crossing Gautama's Ferry, and told how on his last journey north He stood and watched the building of the first of its fortifications, foretelling the future greatness of the capital. In remote villages one constantly comes upon images of Buddha, worshipped inside or outside the temples of Brahman priests. In any field the peasant ploughing may turn up a relic or a fragment of carved stone. And under trees and bushes along the high-road one notes the three little heaps of mud standing side by side, that indicate a shrine of Jaganath the Lord of the Universe, name and symbol of Buddha himself. They have forgotten Him maybe, yet remember His memory, these simple worshippers of the Behari villages. To far distant lands, and to scriptures written in a long-forgotten tongue, the modern organisation of scholarship has to go, to bring back to them the knowledge of Him whom under obscure names they worship to this day, in the very countryside where He lived and taught. A vague tradition of Infinite Mercy is all that remains amongst the unlearned of that wondrous personality. But this, after two thousand years, they cherish still. He belongs in a special degree to this peasantry of Magadha. There runs in their veins the blood of those whom He patted on the head as children. He taught them the dignity of man. He called upon them, as upon the proudest of his peers, to renounce, and find peace in the annihilation of Self. To Gautama Buddha the peasant of Behar owes his place in Hinduism. By him he was nationalised.

Even in those stories of Buddha which remain to us it is explicitly stated that He sought amongst all existing solutions for the truth. This is the meaning of his travelling with the five ascetics and torturing the body with fasts. The first effort of a new thinker must always be to recapitulate existing systems and sound them to their depths. The Prince Gautama in the year 590 B.C., in the populous districts of the Sakya kingdom, awakening suddenly to the sense of his own infinite compassion, and to the career of a world-thinker, feels an overpowering need to meet with the scholars of his age, and makes his way therefore towards the neighbourhood of Rajgir in the kingdom of Magadha. From purely geographical considerations, we can see that there was doubtless another culture-centre, even so early as the age in question, at Taxila, in the extreme north-west. Indeed, towards the end of the life of Buddha himself, we are told of a lad who went there from Magadha—as European students of the Middle Ages to Cordova—to study medicine.

It is also easy to infer that the learning which could be acquired at Taxila was somewhat cosmopolitan in its character. The knowledge of herbs is a comparative science, and Taxila was on the high-road to Persepolis and Babylon, as well as to China and Nineveh. It was the doorway of India, or at least the university which had grown up beside that doorway; and that it was known as such among other nations is shown by the fact that Alexander came that way in 326 B.C. For the purchase of foreign stuffs, for knowledge of the geography that lay beyond her own border, for foreign news and foreign learning, possibly even for secular science as a whole, India had no centre like Taxila.

It follows with equal clearness that for the headquarters of a strictly national culture one would look nearer to the valley of the Ganges. Even the least organised of systems will somewhere have its central ganglion, and the fact that the Indian gangion lay two centuries later in Magadha, is proved by the retirement of Chandra Gupta to Pataliputra after his defeat of the Greeks.

It was evidently not absurd with the means then

at the disposal of the crown to look from that distance to mobilise armies on the frontier. But if military plans could be carried out so far from their base as this, then we cannot object that Magadha was too remote to be the religious centre of the whole. Benares and Baidyanath are still left at its two extremes to tell us of the spiritual energy of its great period. The miracle that puzzles the imagination of historians—the sudden inception in the sixth century B.C. of religions of conscience in place of religions of power is, rightly viewed, no miracle at all. These religions themselves were always there; it was only their organisation that began with the date named.

The events of history follow sequences as rigid as the laws of physics. Buddha was the first of the faith-organisers, and first in India of nation-builders. But Buddha could not rise and do his work until the atmosphere about him had reached a certain saturation-point in respect to those ideas which the Upanishads preach. The founders of religions never create the ideas they enforce. With deep insight they measure their relative values, they enumerate and regiment them; and by the supreme appeal of their own personality they give them a force and vitality unsuspected. But the ideas themselves were already latent in the minds of their audience. Had it not been so, the preacher would have gone uncomprehended. Through how many centuries had this process of democratising the culture of the Upanishads gone on? Only by flashes and side-gleams, as it were, can we gather even the faintest idea.

It is partly the good and partly the bad fortune of Buddhistic movements in India that, from their association with an overwhelming individualised religious idea, they appear to us as a sudden invention of the human mind in such and such a year. We do not sufficiently realise that they, together with all the words and symbols associated with them, must have been taken from a pre-existent stock of customs and expressions already long familiar to the people amongst whom Buddhism grew up. We imagine the great Chandra Gupta to have been the first monarch in India of an organised empire, but the words of Buddha himself, "They build the stupa over a Chakravarti Raja—a suzerain monarch—at a place where four roads meet," show that the people of that early period were familiar enough with the drama of the rise and fall of empires, and that the miracle of Chandra Gupta's retirement to Pataliputra, thence to rule as far as the Punjab and the Indian Ocean, was in fact no miracle at all, since the India of his time was long used to the centralised organisation of roads, *dâks*, and supplies, and to the maintenance of order and discipline.

The peculiar significance of Behar in the comity of the Indian peoples rises out of its position on the frontier-line between two opposing spiritual influences. To this day it is the meeting-place of Hinduistic and Mussulmân civilisations. Sikh and

Arya Somaji and Hindusthani Rajput pour down the waterway of the Ganges, to go no farther east than the twin-cities of Patna and Bankipore, and these stand face to face with the unified and Sanskritic civilisation of Lower Bengal. All sorts of modified institutions, representing mutual assimilation, arise along the border-line. Costume, language, manners, and habits of life are all full of this compromise. The old standard of culture, which even yet is not wholly dead, along a line stretching from Patna through Benares to Lucknow, required of the highest classes of Hindus the study of Persian as well as Sanskrit, and one of the most liberal and courtly types of gentlehood that the world has seen was moulded thus.

The fertile country of Bengal, closely settled and cultivated, organised round the monarchy of Gour, and claiming a definite relation to Benares and Kanauj as the sources of its culture, cannot, at any time within the historical period, have been susceptible of chaotic invasion or colonisation. The drift of unorganised races could never pass through Behar, which must always have been and remains to the present the most cosmopolitan province of India. It has doubtless been this close contiguity of highly-diversified elements within her boundaries that has so often made Behar the birthplace of towering political geniuses. The great Chandra Gupta, his grandson Asoka, the whole of the Gupta dynasty, Shere Shah, and finally Guru Govind Singh, are more than a fair share of the critical personalities of Indian history for one comparatively small district to have produced. Each of the great Beharis has been an organiser. Not one has been a blind force, or the tool of others. Each has consciously surveyed and comprehended contemporary conditions, and known how to unify them in himself, and to give them a final irresistible impulsion in a true direction.

THE ANCIENT ABBEY OF AJANTA[1]

I

LIKE the curves and columns of some great organ runs the line of stone arches and colonnades along the hillside that faces to the sunrise in the glen of Ajanta. Twenty-six caves there are in all, making one long level line, overhung by the rounded ridge of dark-blue stone that was undoubtedly chipped into shape and bareness long long ago to emphasize that balanced uniformity which gives to this ancient abbey so much of its solemnity and beauty. As we first see the caves, from the boulder-strewn stream some hundreds of feet away, they appear

[1] *Chaitya*—Building used by Buddhist monks for united worship; strictly comparable to Christian churches, which resemble it to an extraordinary degree even now. The differences between nave and aisles are exactly the same. A dagoba occupied the place of the altar. Ajanta has four chaityas.

Vihara—A Buddhist monastery. At first these consisted of a central space of irregular shape, with small cells opening into it. Afterwards it becomes a quadrangle or main court with a great sanctuary on its longest side containing an image of Buddha, pillared aisles, verandah, and cells, as in the earlier examples. There are twenty-two viharas, many unfinished, at Ajanta.

Dagoba—A stupa or tope erected over the ashes or relics of a great teacher. An open-air stupa is the Sanchi Tope. There are dagobas within all the four chaityas at Ajanta. Evidently the form was sacred.

GENERAL VIEW OF AJANTA CAVES

like a succession of pillared verandahs, broken once near the middle, and culminating in the distance in the tall arched fronts of great chaitya-halls. It is thus that we first become aware of Caves Ten and Twenty-six, and are affected by their severity and regularity as if by music. In reality, Nine and Nineteen are also chaityas. But both are slightly masked by masses of rock, and only Ten and Twenty-six stand out in this first view.

How lonely and remote is this glen in which we find them! It lies crescent-shaped among its hills, so that the view from each monastery-cave seems closed upon itself. The torrent that runs through it enters, as a great cascade, at the northern end, and leaves this rocky ravine without giving a hint of a world without, where twistings and windings are to bring it to a wider stream. Such are the sites that have ever seemed ideal to the monk. The murmur of running waters and the voices of the waterfalls make to his ear a perpetual plain-song, in unison with the intoning of ancient psalters and the chanting of texts. In the circling path of the sunlight measured against the green, its first rays at dawn and its last at cowdust, are signals for ringing of bells and lighting of lamps, for processions, and incense, and sprinkling of holy water. The quivering of leaves through the tropical day speaks of coolness and shadow, the environment of learning; and the solitude of nature promises remoteness from the world, the only possible environment of holiness. Such must

Ajanta have seemed to the handful of monks who took up their abode in its natural caverns, perhaps a couple of centuries before Asoka. The rough path by which they could climb to their eagle's nests of dwellings was soon hewn by their patient hands into simple stairs. But even these were reached, from the north, only after arduous travel over the boulders by the stream side. A perfect site for a monstery. It is difficult to imagine that amongst the scarped and rugged hillsides of Khandesh there could have been found another vale at once so lonely and so beautiful.

Twenty-six caves there are in all; numbered, in the unemotional fashion of official surveys, in serial order from north to south. In reality, however, they fall according to their ages into some four main groups. The first of these, containing Caves Eight to Thirteen, lies to the left of the stairs by which one reaches the monastery terrace. One arrives on that level between Six and Seven, and the first seven numbers form the third of the periods. Caves Fourteen to Nineteen constitute the second period; and Twenty to Twenty-six the fourth. Thus:—

13, 12, 11, 10, 9, 8: Period I.
19, 18, 17, 16, 15, 14: Period II.
7, 6, 5, 4, 3, 2, 1: Period III.
26, 25, 24, 23, 22, 21, 20: Period IV.

Not that all the caves of any single group were undertaken at once. In each period there is a

AJANTA: FRONT OF CAVE NINETEEN

progression. Sixteen and Seventeen have inscriptions which, it is said, render them the heart of the matter; for they were built during or soon after the lifetime of the great Gupta, Maharaja Deva (Chandragupta II. Vikramaditya, A.D. 375 to 413), by a sovereign who had married his daughter. And Caves Five to One were probably undertaken immediately after.

In any case, it is the first group, Caves Eight to Thirteen, that for hundreds of years formed the whole glory of Ajanta. Eight and Thirteen may probably have been natural caverns occupied tentatively long before the time of Asoka by a handful of monks. Those were days in which kings, rich cities, and great landowners could scarcely perform a work of greater merit than hewing out caves for the residence of monks. In course of time, therefore, these natural recesses in the rock (which we imagine to have been the motive and starting-point) were transformed into simple monasteries by first enlarging the centre and then cutting tiny cells, each with its two stone beds and low doorway, round the space, which thus acted as quadrangle or courtyard. Number Thirteen has, in addition to these, a small earthen verandah in front. Number Eight has not even this. It seems probable that the occupation began from two points more or less simultaneously, and afterwards worked inwards, for how else are we to explain the fact that Nine and Ten, standing side by side, are both chaityas?

We imagine too that the first settlement was early, when faith was strong, and the living impress of the Great Teacher was yet fresh. For how else can we account for the strength that clung to the bare rocks by the torrent-side with such pertinacity, decade after decade? Were they some band of wandering teachers, we wonder, those first monks, appointed to preach in the countries on the Southern Road, a mission sent to the powerful empire of Ujjain, or an offshoot perhaps from the mother-communities at Bhilsa and Sanchi? In any case, the caves were valuable to them as headquarters during the wet season, when all begging friars are supposed to assemble for the time in some fixed dwelling-place; and during their absences as a body, for eight or nine months at a time, the work of excavation must have gone forward. Little did they dream of how well-starred were both the spot they had chosen and the day of their advent! We can see, what they could not, close on twelve hundred years of development and gathering fame, the learning they were to send out; the beauty they were to build up; the kings who would delight to honour them; and roads from the far ends of the earth, all meeting on their threshold. Hiouen Tsang came here, in the middle of the seventh century after Christ, and speaks of the place as "a *sangharama* constructed in a dark valley. Its lofty halls and deep side-aisles stretch through the face of the rocks. Storey above storey, they are backed by the crag and face the valley."

It is evident here that the English translator—not having in his own mind the thing his author was describing—has rendered the text inaccurately. If we read, "its lofty chaityas and deep viharas at their sides," the statement immediately becomes luminous. Similarly, when later we are told that the great vihara is about 100 feet high, and the stone figure of Buddha in the middle 70 feet high, while above is a canopy of seven stages, towering upwards, apparently without support,[1] it is evident that the great Chinese traveller is speaking of no vihara, but of the principal chaitya of his own day (Nineteen or Twenty-six?), and that the stone figure he describes is really the dagoba it contains.

The first royal patronage extended to Ajanta must have been given at or soon after the time of Asoka, when the chaitya known as Cave Nine and the vihara numbered Twelve were built. Every one who takes up the study of ancient sites in India finds his own indications of age. At Sanchi the gradual modifications in the pictorial treatment of the Asokan rail give us a chronological scale which enables us to distinguish with absolute certainty no less than four different periods of building and sculpture. Here at Ajanta the time-unit that serves us from the first is the chaitya-façade ornament taken in conjunction with the Asokan rail. It would appear that the domestic architecture of the age was characterised by the rounded roof

[1] Quoted by R. C. Dutt in *Civilisation in Ancient India*, ii. pp. 156–7.

which we still see in the rocky caves of Ajanta; by the Asokan rail, used as the front of a verandah; and by the horse-shoe window, breaking the line of the roof, or mansard. Now the instinct of cave-makers was to make their fronts as closely as possible resemble the outsides of the buildings of their period.

But a style creates a tradition, which persists long after the original reason for it has disappeared. Thus the horse-shoe ornament and the Asokan rail become a mannerism at Ajanta, diverging constantly further and further from their true intention; and by these progressive changes we can make a rough estimate of the ages of the caves. In Nine and Twelve they are used with obvious sincerity, reflecting the conceptions of their age, in the same way that the early printers of Europe laboured to make their machine-printed books look as if they had been written by hand. On viharas Eight and Thirteen they do not occur at all. Evidently the founders were too early or too poor to indulge in such elaboration. Chaitya Number Ten had a timber front, which has fallen away and leaves no trace of its image or likeness, save in the panels sculptured in the rocks on either side. But these horse-shoe ornaments do not altogether cease till after Cave Nineteen. At first they are frankly windows in house fronts. In Cave Twelve. they are to suggest used fan-lights over the cell-doors and run round the walls connecting one with another in simple dignity. In Caves

AJANTA: INTERIOR OF CAVE NINETEEN

Six, Seven, and Fifteen we find the spaces filled with lotus patterns, and the semicircular opening no longer has a definite meaning. They are no longer windows. They are now only decorative. On the façade of Cave Nineteen foreign influences are at work. A horrible vulgarity has come over the workmen, strictly comparable to the degrading effects of European taste on Indian crafts to-day. Each of these once beautiful outlines is now filled with a hideous grinning face, altogether meaningless. From the chequer-work which recurs here again and again (an ornament common amongst the Gandhara sculptures in the Calcutta collection), it is clear that these influences have come from the north-west. They are possibly Greek, as transmitted through Persia. There had been a great *rapprochement* between India and Persia in the course of the fifth century, and nowhere is the crude secularising effect of the West on Indian taste better illustrated.

Yet nowhere is the sober, synthetising power of the Indian intellect more visible. In spite of its eclecticism of detail, and daring romanticism in the treatment of sacred subjects, Nineteen at Ajanta remains one of the architectural triumphs of the world. It is the very flowering-point of a great civic life. The strong porch, brought forward on two solid pillars, suggests the presence and words of the leaders of men ; the side-galleries, their supporters and attendants ; while on the sill of the great window behind we have room and background for the anointing of a king, or the lying-in-state of the dead.

We are accustomed to think of the *hôtels de ville* of Belgium as the crown of the world's communal architecture. But Belgium has nothing, for simple unity and mastery, to compare with this. It dominates a small court, from which a false step would precipitate one down a steep *khud.* Obviously the style was not invented for such a position. Here, as at a thousand other points, Ajanta merely reflects the life of India during one of the greatest periods of her history. Cave Nineteen remains, carved in imperishable rock, when all the buildings of its day have disappeared, a memorial of the splendour and restraint of Indian cities during the ages of the Gupta rule.

II

From the story of the first Council, held at Rajgir in the year following the death of Buddha, we learn that it was usual among the monks to apply for royal aid for the construction and repair of the viharas. It was not the business of the monks themselves to build or to excavate with their own hands; though those amongst them who had in the world been master-craftsmen would undoubtedly organise and direct the labour assigned to the Abbey, as has been the case amongst monastic orders in all lands and in all ages. It is indeed their disinterested co-operation, their giving all and asking nothing in return, that enables an order of monks to create so much that is permanent within a short time. No other industrial unit can be compared with them in their power of accumulating results. And the secret is that the monk's whole purpose is his work itself. Whatever his task, whether building, or education, or manufacture, his ideal requires that he have no motive outside. He subordinates himself to his duty, instead of using it to serve some selfish end. The gain derived from the deed, in means or skill, is used only to make possible some vaster and grander effort of the same kind.

This is why the old abbeys of Europe and their associated churches are so beautiful. They cost nothing like the wealth that went to the making of cathedrals. Standing in remote places, they were built almost entirely by peasant and village-labourer. But every stone was laid under the design and superintendence of the monks themselves. Years of dreaming found expression in groined roofs, clustered pillars, radiating arches; in chantry-niche or holy well or casket-like shrine. The monks themselves were recruited from all classes of the population, but, on the face of it, we might expect that a smith or a carpenter who chose the religious life would be distinguished by somewhat more of thought and organising powers, more of idealism and more of dreams, than the brothers he had left at the anvil or the bench.

This law, exemplified in Europe, is as true of

India. It characterises all monastic orders everywhere. It is in the very nature of the monastic idea, and nowhere have we a better opportunity of watching its action than at Ajanta. For the Buddhist orders, like those of Europe, were democratic. No stain or fetter of birth barred entrance into them. The *sramanas,* unlike the *Brahmanas,* testified Megasthenes three and a half centuries before Christ, are not born to their condition, but are taken from all classes of the population. Thus they represented the whole national life of their time, and we owe the beauty of their architecture to the taste and imagination of the monks themselves.

But we must remember that for command of means the monks depended upon neighbouring kings and cities. It was an act of surpassing merit to excavate caves or adorn chaitya-halls for religious communities. Kings remitted the taxes of whole villages, which thus became the monastery glebe. Noblemen and great ministers devoted vast sums to the making of images, cloisters, and shrines. There is an inscription in the Kuda Caves[1] which shows that a whole family of king's officers, including the daughters-in-law, joined to contribute the expenses of the various definite items necessary for the making of a Buddha chapel. In the *karma* thus accumulated not one of this loving and obedient group must be left out. Here at Ajanta itself Cave Sixteen is made by a minister

[1] A place 45 miles south of Bombay. Very early caves.

AJANTA: SCULPTURE IN CAVE TWENTY

of the Vakataka princes known as Varahadeva; Caves Seventeen, Eighteen, and Nineteen by a minister of a tributary sovereign or great noble called Aditya; Cave Twenty by a man of evident wealth and distinction, whose name is Upendra Gupta; and the chaitya hall, Cave Twenty-six, by the abbot Buddha Bhadra with the special assistance of his subordinate Dharmadatta and his own disciple Bhadra Bandhu.

Throughout the west country it was long fashionable, even for houses that were themselves devoted to Shiva or to Vishnu, to make these benefactions to the Buddha friars. And as time went on it became customary to add an inscription, with the prayer that the merit of the act might redound to the benefit first of the father and mother of the donor, and then of all living beings—a dedication that is still common amongst certain Buddhist peoples.

From Caves Sixteen and Seventeen, then, it can hardly be doubted that the great power within whose territory Ajanta lay was that of the Vakataka princes, whose sway is supposed on other grounds to have covered a large part of Central India, from the end of the third till the middle of the sixth centuries, their dynasty having been powerful enough to take a queen from the family of the great Chandra Gupta of Pataliputra, between A.D. 420 and 490.[1]

[1] It is absurd to suppose that "the great king of kings, Devagupta," has any other meaning.

Who were these Vakatakas? Where did they reign? What was the nature of their kingdom and their power? The inscription on Cave Sixteen claims that Harisena, the king under whom both it and Seventeen were excavated (A.D. 500 to 520), had conquered amongst other places Ujjain, Orissa, and Kosala. Are we to suppose from this that they were Rajputs reigning in Malwa, that country of which Hiouen Tsang said a century later that it could only be compared with Magadha as the home of learning? And were the tributary Asmakas—whose minister Aditya made Seventeen, Eighteen, and Nineteen—a mere local power, confined to the immediate neighbourhood? How urgently the history of India calls for students who will search it out in the light of its geography! An anxious antiquarianism has been very useful in providing a few data and starting-points for real work. But the day has come when we are able to realise that, except as the great stream of the Indian story carries it, even Ajanta has little value. We must know how it stood related to the life of its period; what it did for the world; who loved and served it; what joy they drew from it; and a thousand other truths about that living past which surrounded its birth. No one has yet troubled to depict the social conditions out of which it grew. Yet this is the very thing that we must know. The network of strong cities that must have surrounded every focus of ecclesiastical power and learning is non-existent as yet in the national imagination. Yet only a detailed study of the whole countryside can give us the real clue to the development of sites like Ajanta.

We forget that every age seems modern to itself, and that warm throbbing human life once filled these empty cells, that human love and conviction inspired every line and curve of their contour, and that human thought beat ceaselessly to and fro against their walls and screens in its search to determine for man the grounds of eternal certainty. But even when we have answered these questions we have yet to answer one other, as pressing, as important. How did all this activity come to an end? The history of the death of Buddhism in India has yet to be entered upon, in the true spirit of critical inquiry; but when it is undertaken, what vast areas will be found elucidated!

Here in the neighbourhood of Ajanta are many features of interest and possible significance. The railway is still forty miles away, and has not yet had time to derange the commercial relations of the grand old market town called Neri, encircled by its battlemented walls. Some eight miles to the north of the caves lies the postal town of Vakod. Is there any connection here with the word *Vakataka?* Four miles to the south on one side, and again four to the north on the other, are the towns of Ajanta and Fardapur. Both are seats of Moghul fortification testifying to the strong and independent character of the country from early times. At Ajanta there is a palace and a bridge of some ten arches, with an enclosed pool, below which lie the seven cascades that lead to the monastic ravine.

In the grim old village of Fardapur there is another fort of Aurungzeb, which is now in use as a caravanserai. The whole aspect of the place is ancient and fortress-like, and the mode of building which obtains there throws a sudden light on what must have been the aspect of Rajgir, when Buddha entered it, in the days of Bimbisara five and six centuries before Christ. Every wall has a basis of pebbles and mortar; and upon this are reared blocks of baked earth, shaped like masses of masonry. They are broad at the base, considerably narrower at the top, and the slope from one to the other is slightly concave. Even the delicate brick battlements of the Moghuls are built upon an older foundation of rubble wall. A similar mode of shaping earth obtains even so far east, it is said, as the western districts of Bengal. Undoubtedly it is a method of unknown antiquity. The curving slant gives to every cottage the air of a fortification, which indeed it is, and from a mediæval point of view a fortification of very admirable materials.

Even had the old walls of the fort not been visible under the Moghul battlements, we should have known that the place represented an ancient camp of the people, rather than the mere stronghold of an army of occupation. This is shown, in the first place, by its size. It is, in fact, a walled court or compound, containing a spring of water and a place of worship. Around it are quarters for hundreds of people, and at the gateways and corner-towers residences for officers. A whole population could take refuge here with their women and their cows against the onset of an army or the invasion of a tribe. The fact that it could have been worth while for a powerful government like that of Delhi to occupy so large a work at the close of the Dekkan wars, in what seems to us now an obscure village, is a wonderful testimony to the strength and hostility of the Mahratta country round it, a strength and hostility which were the expression of thousands of years of organised independence.

Outside the fort the city has been walled, and the river, circling within the walls, has acted at the gateway of the city as a moat, over which even now stand the ruins of a grand old bridge of three arches. At the end of the road that once crossed this bridge, at what must have been the outer gate of the city, there is a buttress-foundation, now treated as a sacred mound, where both Hindus and Mohammedans come to worship the Mother. The trees that grow on it are the *neem* and the *bo*, the old *bodhi*-tree, or *asvattha*. At their feet a few stones are red with vermilion, and broken glass bracelets tell of accepted vows.

So much for the mingling of historic and prehistoric. All through this countryside we find ourselves close to the remoter origins of Hinduism.

It is a land of the worship of Miri-Amma, the Earth-Mother, in her symbols of the *neem* and the pointed stone. There are temples of Hanuman too here and there. But though I found a Brahman chanting the worship of Satyanarayan in his own house on the full-moon night I saw no shrines to Shiva or Vishnu. This *bo*-tree on the Ajanta road may have sheltered a friars' *dharmsala* in Buddhistic ages. Here at this gate Hiouen Tsang and his train, in the middle of the seventh century, may have stopped to pay toll or to rest, on their way to or from the abbey, four miles distant. And the *bo*-tree, growing here beside the *neem*, may seem to the spirit of the place, with the memories it recalls of the peopled cloisters of twelve hundred years ago, a memento of what is a comparatively recent incident in the long long story of the land.

Hinayana and Mahayana

Buddhism might well be divided historically by the students into the Rajgir, the Pataliputra, and the Takshasila periods. Or we might choose for the names of our periods those monarchs who were the central figures of each of these epochs. At Rajgir these would be Bimbisara and his son Ajatasatru, at Pataliputra Asoka, and at Takshasila Kanishka, the second sovereign of the Kushan empire. The epochs thus named would also be coterminous with the dates of the three great

Buddhist Councils. No complete history of Buddhism could leave out of account the influence of the great Kanishka. For from his time, as we are informed by the Chinese travellers, dates that great schism of the Mahayana, or Northern School, which has carried with it China, Japan, and Tibet, while Burma, Ceylon, and Siam belong to Southern Buddhism, or the Lesser Vehicle.

A great haughtiness divides to this day the adherents of these different schools. To the Northern School belongs the new recension of the scriptures published by the Council of Kanishka. To the Southern belong the simpler and more ancient works, amongst which are included the three Tripitakas.

The characteristic doctrine of the Mahayana, according to the disciples of Hiouen Tsang in the early eighth century, lies in the veneration of the Bodhisattvas, along with the one earthly and supreme Buddha. The Southern School, or Hinayana, does not profess to invoke the Bodhisattvas. But it is easy to see that under this brief definition there is indicated a wide divergence of attitudes and teaching. Anyone who studies a religious movement which has its origin in an Indian and Hinduistic teacher, is bound to notice two opposite influences which come into play almost simultaneously. First there is the highly abstract and nihilistic character of the personal realisation of the Master himself. No gods, no forms, no rites, and the unreal and phenomenal nature of the world about him, all this is the immediate and strongest impression made on the mind. Heaven must not be thought of, perfection is the only possible goal for the soul. And so on. But at the selfsame moment, by creating a profound sympathy for India, and the Indian way of looking at the world, the door is opened to all sorts of complexities, and the disciple may well end by accepting a thousand things, each as unthinkable as the one or two he originally abandoned at the call of a higher truth. Such must always be the twofold effect of an Indian teacher of religion on a foreign mind.

This very phenomenon we may watch on a geographical scale in the history of Buddhism. Here the Southern countries, served by the early missions, received a stricter and more personal impress of the deposit of faith actually left to his church by the Master. This system was atheistic, nihilistic, and philosophic in the highest and severest sense. Even in the reign of Asoka we see the erection of rails, pillars, and stupas, the glorification of holy places, and the worship of the sacred relics, but never a trace of the multitudinous extraneous elements which were later to be accepted.

Many of the great chaitya halls were built between the time of Asoka and the Christian era, but the stupas which they contain are simple reliquaries. The dagoba bears no image, though it is often ornamented with an Asokan rail. Sculpture was in existence at this early date, but it seems to have been used always as a medium of secular commemoration, as at Karli and Bharhut. The religious symbolism of Buddhistic devotion seems to have been at this period the tree, the stupa, the rail, the horse-shoe ornament, and sometimes a footprint. Nor can we adequately realise the thrill of sympathy and reverence which these austere and simple forms were at that time capable of producing in a susceptible mind.

The recognition of the Bodhisattvas, however, which came in with Kanishka, is a phrase which covers a great deal. It really connoted sooner or later the acceptance more or less entire of what may be called the Asiatic synthesis. And it too seems to go hand in hand with the worship of the personality of Buddha himself. It was in fact the emergence of a doctrine for which India has ever since been famous. It was an outbreak of the tendency known in Christianity as the religion of the Incarnation, a form of adoration by which Protestant England herself has wellnigh been torn in twain during the last fifty years. Whether or not Buddhism had before this inculcated the adoration of the Buddha's personality, no one who has read any of the early scriptures can doubt that she was always very ready for such a doctrine. There is a fine sentiment about every mention of the Teacher's name. One can feel the intense sacredness of each of his movements to the early recorder. And the worship of relics, so early as the moment of the Mahanirvana itself, is an evidence not to be set aside. The doctrine of the divinity of Buddha and his miraculous birth into a world long preparing for his advent must in the year A.D. 150 have been only the keystone of an arch already built. Here we have the picture of the self-projection into the sphere of *maya* of a soul immeasurably higher and sweeter than those dragged there by their own deeds. It is the theory which reappears in widely separate times and places under the names of Christ, Rama, Krishna, and Chaitanya. Even the Persian Bab would seem to owe the idea that makes him possible to this Indian "superstition," as it has been called.

This was the movement that placed in each new vihara excavated at Ajanta its Buddha shrine. Whether Seven or Eleven is the older it is difficult to determine, but each contains its image in its shrine. This fact coincides with a further step taken about this time. The ancient abbey with its *bhikshugrihas* began to transform itself into a university. Each of these new and more ambitious viharas is a college as well as a monastery. We are very familiar, from the study of Burma and Japan, with the educational system in which every student is theoretically a novice of the monastery. Something of the same sort is true to this day of Oxford itself. And there can be no doubt that it obtained at Ajanta. It was with this emphasizing of the function of the *sangharama* as the abode of learning that the image of the great teacher became all-important. For organised worship the chaitya halls always sufficed. The image in its shrine doubtless received a certain ritualised attention morning and evening—above all, incense was burnt before it—but its main purpose was to keep the students in mind of the great Guru, the divine teacher and ideal, in whose invisible presence every act was to be performed. It is this academic aspect of the life at Ajanta which speaks in the long rows of viharas dug out within single epochs. The numbers Four to One cannot be far removed from number Seventeen, and this fact can only be accounted for in this way. Of the learning that was imparted in these monastic colleges we read in Hiouen Tsang. From the beginning the texts must have been recited constantly in the abbey-halls. But that secular learning also was sometjmes cultivated we are expressly told in the case of Nalanda, where arithmetic and astronomy were studied, and standard time was kept for the kingdom of Magadha by means of the state water-clock.

Not all the sculptural developments of Ajanta are Kanishkan. The façade of Cave Nineteen, of some centuries later, shows in a wonderful manner the richness and variety of the elements to which the Mahayana had opened the door. Buddha is there treated not simply as the guru whose every trace and footstep is sacred, but as a great historic character, to be portrayed in many ways and from many different points of view. He is being crowned. He carries the flag of Dharmma. There is a freedom in his attitudes and in the arrangement of the adoring figures by whom he is surrounded. At the same time, the recurrence of the chequer-pattern instead of the Asokan rail, now forgotten, shows the influence of Gandhara. And so the substitution of grinning faces for lotuses in the horse-shoe ornaments shows the overwhelming of the old purely Indian impulse by foreign influences. And so does the peculiar coat worn by the Buddhas. This garment appears to me rather Chinese or Tartar than West Asian. But it must be said that it is not purely Indian. What is the date of Cave Nineteen? Kanishka was A.D. 150, or thereabouts, and Cave Seventeen is about A.D. 520. It is customary to assume that Nineteen is the Gandakuti or image-house referred to in the inscription on Seventeen. Critics profess to find an affinity of style which groups them together. For my own part I must frankly say that to me this affinity is lacking. I believe the Gandakuti to mean the image shrine at the back of Seventeen itself. A pious founder might well count this and the cave and the cistern three separate works. This inference is confirmed by a reference I find in Hiouen Tsang to a *gandakuti* or hall of perfumes, *i.e.* doubtless, of incense *within* a vihara in the kingdom of Takka. I cannot imagine that Nineteen was made by the same hands or at the same time as Seventeen. I think it is considerably later and less conservative and exclusively Indian. At the same time I think it must be the "great vihara" of Hiouen Tsang, which he describes as about 100 feet high, while in the midst is a stone figure of Buddha about 70 feet high, and above this a stone canopy of seven stages, towering upwards apparently without any support. Making allowance for faulty translation in regard to terms, which by those who have seen the caves are used with technical rigidity, this may offer a fair description of the cave as it would appear to one who saw it in the plenitude of its use and beauty. If this cave were, as I think, excavated about the year A.D. 600, then when the Chinese traveller visited the abbey in the middle of the century it would be the central place of worship and one of the main features of interest at Ajanta. But there is at least one other synchronism of the greatest significance to be observed in reference to Cave Nineteen. This is the affinity of the treatment of Buddha in its sculptures to those of Borobuddor in Java. It is as if the style were only making its first appearance. There is the same idea of costume, and the standing Buddhas have something like the same grace of attitude and gentleness of demeanour, but the process of idealising has not yet been carried to its highest pitch in this kind. There is in the Javanese Buddhas, as revealed in Mr. Havell's photographs of them, an ethereal remoteness with which these do not quite compete. Yet here is the promise of it. And the great bas-relief on the stupa in the interior has the same look, is of the same quality. The expedition that colonised Java is said to have left Gujarat in western India early in the seventh century, and this was evidently the conception of fine art that they carried away with them.

In this visit of Hiouen Tsang to the abbey, we have a hint of the marvellous cosmopolitanism which probably characterised its life. It is another way of saying the same thing, that is said with almost equal distinctness, by the chaitya-façade itself. Chinese, Gandharan, Persian, and Ceylonese elements mingle with touches from every part of India itself in the complexity of this superb edifice. The jewel-like decorations of the columns without remind us of Magadha. The magnificent pillars inside carry the mind to Elephanta and its probably Rajput dynasty. The very ornate carvings of the triforium and the pillar-brackets were originally plastered and coloured. The stupa also once blazed with chunam and pigments. The interior must have been in accord therefore with the taste of an age that was by no means severe. The Vakataka house must have ruled over an empire in Middle India in which civilisation had reached a very high level. It must have been the centre of free and healthy communications with foreign powers. And above all, the old international life of learning must have had full scope in the abbey's hospitality. Buddha and the Bodhisattvas were only the outstanding figures in a divine world which included a constantly-growing number of factors. The little choultry outside is purely Hinduistic in its sculpture, as if to say that the order looked with no unfriendly eye on the less organised religious ideas and affections of the pilgrim householder. A mythological system which is practically identical in Japan, China, and India sheltered itself behind the Mahayana. All the sacred and learned literature of India was by it put in a position of supremacy. Hiouen Tsang was as careful to pass on to his disciples the comments of Panini on Sanskrit grammar as more strictly theological lore. He was as eager for the explanation of Yoga—the secular science of that age—as for the clearing up of points about relics and shrines. India, in fact, as soon as the Mahayana was formulated, entered on a position of undisputed pre-eminence as the leader and head of the intellectual life of Asia.

The Theory of Greek Influence on Indian Art

Nothing is clearer at Ajanta than the existence of two separate and almost divergent ways of treating the Buddha. One of these we see in the Buddha of the Shrines, which represents the moment of the First Sermon at Benares. Buddha is seated on his throne, and *devas* are flying into the halo behind his head. On the predella below his seat are the symbolic animals, and in their midst the Wheel of the Law. The dress of the Master is the Indian *chudder* of fine white muslin. And in some form or other there is always a suggestion of the lotus in the throne, although it may take the form of folds of drapery. In all these respects we have a very distinct approach to the type of Buddha which is fixed in our minds as representative of Sarnath and also of Sanchi. The face here is characterised by a much greater masculinity than that of Sarnath—whose ostentatious technical perfection shows it to be a late example of the style—but there are all the same elements in the composition as a whole: the flying devas, the wheel, the lotus, and the halo; and the dress is of the same fine and barely visible order. In Cave Fifteen, especially, a greatly heightened beauty is obtained by the fact that the halo is detached from the head of the figure, thus producing a shadow, which gives an air of life and freedom to the statue. This is only one out of many signs that the type is not rigidly fixed, but is to be seen at Ajanta as at Sanchi or Sarnath itself, playing round a general symbolistic convention. This Buddha is integral to Caves Seven, Eleven, Fifteen, Sixteen, and Seventeen, at any rate; and that these caves precede Cave Nineteen in date there can be no doubt. A similar type of Buddha is also integral to the series of Caves numbered Six to One, but since it is probable that these were excavated after Seventeen, we dare not base upon them any argument which might depend upon their being anterior to Nineteen. Therefore, we shall here rely upon the Sarnath Buddha, as found during the evolution of the type, in Caves Eleven to Seventeen only.

With Cave Nineteen we come suddenly upon a new type. Here the Buddha on the great dagoba is standing in what is now commonly known as the teaching attitude; though in truth the monks and their students who used the viharas, probably thought of the attitude of the First Sermon as that of the teaching Buddha. Be this as it may, the standing Buddha of the dagoba is clothed in a *choga* over and above his muslin underclothing. And this *choga* is not unlike the garment also to be found on the gold coins of Kanishka. It is in truth a yellow *robe,* and not merely the yellow *cloth,* of the Buddhist monk. It is in any case a clear and indubitable sign of the intercourse between Ajanta and the colder regions of north-western India, and marks the influence of the latter at this particular moment upon the Buddhist symbolism of Central India. This influence is borne out in many ways by subordinate evidence, into which we need not enter at present. The point now is, Had India already owed the idea of the Sarnath Buddha itself to this same stream of north-west influence on her arts?

Ordinarily speaking, we are accustomed to take for granted that an artistic style has arisen more or less in the neighbourhood of the place in which we find it. It requires no argument to convince us that Velasquez was the product of Spain or Titian of Venice. Even if we had not been informed of this we should have assumed it. To this rule, however, India has so far been an exception. The synthetic study of her past suffers from having been largely initiated by foreigners. The modern method has been forced upon the country from outside, and it is difficult for outsiders to believe that the same thing has not happened before, that it is not indeed somewhat distinctive of Indian development. The German scholar Grünwedel, writing on Buddhist art, reiterates his sincere conviction over and over again that India derives her new impulses from foreign sources. Fergusson, with the prepossessions of his long work for Indian architecture fresh upon him, finds more difficulty in minimising the purely native elements in Buddhist art, and though not untouched, is yet vastly less impressed by the pre-eminence of Gandhara types, when he comes upon them, than are his successors. And perhaps it is useful to know that neither of these writers is so assured of the negligibility of the indigenous contributions to Buddhistic symbolism as the latest of all, Mr. Vincent Smith, in his Early History of India. This is worth mentioning, because it may serve to remind us that even in a matter which has seemed so fixed and determined as this of the Gandharan influence on Buddha types, we really have to deal rather with a strong and cumulative drift of opinion or prejudice or preconception—as we may choose to call it—than with established facts. Vincent Smith is not better able to form an opinion than Fergusson. Indeed he is less fit in many ways; yet his opinion is much more fixed. What the one man threw out as a tentative suggestion the other uses as if it were an axiom. Evidently even the best of us is apt to believe as he would wish, or as he has prepared himself to think, and there is a large fraction of predisposition in every robust conviction. Therefore the formidable concensus of opinion which at present exists on the origin of Buddhist iconography, does not in the least exonerate us from examining carefully the grounds of that opinion. On the contrary, it rather challenges us to do so. Of the three famous names cited, it is precisely that of the man who knew his India best which is also that of him who attaches least importance to foreign influences in Buddhist art. And it is the man who knows least of Indian art at first hand, and is presumably most influenced by popular opinion, who delivers it over most cheerfully to a foreign origin and the assumption of native inadequacy and incompetence.

There are two different theories about foreign influence on the Indian art of the Buddhist period. One is that from the beginning India had owed almost everything artistic to external forces. The Asokan pillars were Persepolitan, the winged animals were Assyrian, the very lotuses and plant-forms were West-Asian. The school which thus almost holds that India has no originality in matters of art, leans its own weight for the sources of her Buddhistic inspiration on the existence in Bactria, ever since the time of Alexander, of Greek artisan colonies. From these descendants of Greek settlers sprang the art of India. And what was not communicated thus had been the gift of Persia to the East. These two sources being postulated, we may accept the whole story of India's greatness in matters artistic without doubt and without distress.

The other theory bears more especially and definitely on the evolution of the statue of Buddha as a sacred image. This, it is held, was not an Indian invention. The idea was first conceived in the country of Gandhara, the contact-point between India and the West. Here, between the beginning of the Christian era and the year A.D. 540, when they were broken up by the tyrant Mihirakula, there was a very rich development of Buddhism in the form of stupas and monasteries. And the argument of Grünwedel may be accepted with regard to the number of Euro-classical elements which the art of this Buddhistic development displayed. There is to this day a highly artistic population established in the region in question, including as that does Kashmir and the North Punjab, and almost touching Tibet, and on the other side of Afghanistan and Persia. The fertility of the races who meet at this point, in decorative arts and forms of all kinds, need not be disputed. Nor would they ever be slow to absorb new elements that might present themselves in unusual abundance at some well-marked political period. The fact that this would surely happen is only part of their extraordinary artistic ability. The conversion of the country of Kashmir to Buddhism would follow naturally on Buddhistic activity in Gandhara, and this was strong between the first century of the Christian era and A.D. 540, and even persisted with modified energy for a couple of centuries longer, as we can gather through Hiouen Tsang. We may also accept without cavil the statement that ever since the raid of Alexander there had been an eastward flowing traffic along the ancient trade-routes that connected India with the West. We cannot admit that Alexander created these routes. That had been done silently through the ages that preceded him by the footsteps of merchants and pilgrims, of traders and scholars, and even monks. The fame of Indian philosophy in the West had preceded Alexander. Indian thinkers had long gone, however few and far between, in the wake of Indian merchants. But it is possibly true that before the raid there had been very little compensating back-flow into India. The great geographical unity and distinctness of this country must be held, if so, to account for the phenomenon. India was the terminus of at least one line of international travel in an eastern direction. Undoubtedly the overland route of those days was still more vigorously followed up under the Roman Empire. It was to India with her advanced civilisation that the Roman Empire went for its luxuries, and Pliny laments the drain of imperial gold for the silks and ivory and gems of the East. The finding of many obviously Greek relics, such as a Silenus, and Heracles with the Nemæan lion, at Mathura, would seem to indicate that the older trade-routes had come in by sea, and ended at that city, in the interior of the country, on the river Jumna. But the roads that ended in Gandhara, and brought the influences of classical Europe to bear on Buddhism there, were certainly those which connected it with the old Byzantium and with Rome. Greek art may have spoken at Mathura, but certainly nothing better than the Græco-Roman ever made itself felt in the north-west. All this represents facts which will be acknowledged. The argument that the artistic capacities of the Gandharan region in the time of the Roman Empire were the result of a certain ethnic strain, due to Alexander and the Græco-Bactrian kingdom which succeeded him, is not of a character to be taken very seriously. Garrisons of occupation are not usually accompanied by the representative genius of their home-countries in such force and numbers as to act with this spiritual intensity on strange populations, partly through personal contacts and partly through mixing of blood! We may compare the assumed achievement with what has been accomplished by modern peoples, under similar circumstances and with vastly superior advantages, if we wish to bring the proposition to its own *reductio ad absurdum*. But in fact it need not be approached so gravely.

Photo: Johnston and Hoffmann

FRESCO DESIGNS OF AJANTA

The best answer to the suggestion lies in the extraordinary difference between the two forms of art. The art of the Greek world was concerned almost entirely with the human form. The horse, indeed, with the deer, the eagle, and the palm-tree, are not altogether unknown to it. But it is remarkable for the absence of any strong feeling for vegetative beauty, or for the animal world as a whole. Now it is precisely in these two elements that the populations of the Gandharan country were and are to this day strongest. Severe chastity and restraint of the decorative instinct is the mark of Greece. Exuberance is the characteristic, on the other hand, of Oriental art. It revels in invention. Its fertility of flower and foliage is unbounded. Being of the nature of high art, it knows indeed how to submit itself to curbing forces. The highest achievement of the Eastern arts of decoration, whether Chinese or Persian, Tibetan or Kashmirian, or Indian proper, often seems to lie in the supreme temperance and distinction with which they are used. But the power of hydra-headed productivity is there. In Greece and Rome it is altogether lacking Thus to say that the art of Gandhara was due to elements in the population which were of Hellenic descent is absurd. There was never in it the slightest sign of any wedding of East and West in a single blended product, such as this theory presupposes. We can always pick out the elements in its compositions that are unassimilated of the West, as well as those that are unassimilated of the East, and those, thirdly, that are purely local and more or less neutral.

The same is true of the Persepolitan pillars and winged animals of the older Mauryan art. Of internationalism these are eloquent, but by no means of intellectual imitation. India, as the producer of so many of the rare and valuable commodities of the world, was the most international of early countries. The positions of her great merchants, such as was that one who excavated the chaitya at Karli, may well have transcended those of kings. Amongst the most important of the world's highways were those that joined Babylon and Nineveh to the Dekkan and to Pataliputra, or Egypt and Arabia to Ceylon and China. It shows the dignity and international standing of India that she should have used freely the best of the age, undeterred by any premature or artificial sense of national boundaries. If we take one group of winged animals quoted by Grünwedel from Sanchi, there is even a kind of accuracy of scholarship in the way these are given foreign men, as riders, in their own dress and with their heraldic devices, so to speak, of the time. Those who incline to think that because she used Persepolitan pillars, therefore she derived her civilisation from West Asia, have to ignore the whole matrix of the original and individual in which such elements inhere. The pillars of the chaitya at Karli may go by the name of Persepolitan, but the idea of the chaitya-hall itself, for which they are utilised, has never been supposed to be anything but Indian. The pillar with a group of animals on the top of it is not, in truth, adapted to the structural uses that it serves at Karli. It is the creation of Asia at an age when pillars were conceived as standing free, to act as landmarks, as vehicles of publication, as memorials of victory, and possibly even as lamp-standards. But this use was common to all Asia, including India, and though the Achamenides adorn Persepolis with it in the sixth century before Christ, and Asoka uses it at Sarnath or at Sanchi in the third, we must remember that the latter is not deliberately copying monuments from a distant site, but is translating into stone a form probably familiar to his people and his age in wood. In the simple chaityas Nine and Ten, at Ajanta—excavated during the same period as Karli, but by simple monks intent upon their use, instead of by a great merchant-prince, with his ecclesiastical ostentation — the columns from floor to roof are of unbroken plainness. The result may lose in vividness and splendour, but it certainly gains in solemnity and appropriateness. And the extremes of both these purposes, we must remember, are of the Indian genius.

Other things being equal, it is to be expected that symbols will emanate from the same sources as ideals. For an instance of this we may look at the European worship of the Madonna. Here it is those churches that create and preach the ideal which are also responsible for the symbolism under which it is conveyed. It would seem indeed as if it were only as the vehicle of the ideal that the symbol could possibly be invented or disseminated. Now if we ask what was the radiating centre for the thought and aspiration of Buddhism, the answer comes back without hesitation or dispute—Magadha. The Holy Land of Buddhism was the stretch of country between Benares and Pataliputra. Here the First Council had been held in the year after Buddha's death, at Rajgir. Here at Pataliputra under Asoka was held the great Second Council about the year 242 B.C. It is quite evident that the lead so well taken by Magadha in recognising the importance of Buddhism during the lifetime of its founder had been signally maintained, and for the Council of Kanishka to assert canonical rank, it must have been attended by numerous and authoritative representatives from the monasteries of Magadha, notably that of Nalanda, whose supremacy as the seat of exposition and elucidation was still acknowledged in the time of Hiouen Tsang in the middle of the seventh century of the Christian era. Unless then there should be unimpugnable evidence to the contrary, the rule being that ideals create symbolisms as their vehicle, and the source of Buddhist thought having always been Magadha, we should expect that that country would also be the creative centre in matters of Buddhist art, and that it would be responsible amongst other things for the devising and fixing of the image of Buddha. That this was the common belief on the matter in the seventh century, moreover, appears highly probable from the Life of Hiouen Tsang, whose biographer and disciple Hwui Li represents him as bearing back to China, and passing through the country of Takkha or Gandhara on the way, a precious load of books and images, and amongst these first, and evidently most sacred and important, that of Buddha preaching his First Sermon at Benares, fully described. From this it is clear that in China, in the seventh century at all events, India was regarded as the source of authentic images as well as of authoritative texts and their interpretations. To India, and more especially to Magadha, the East turned again and again to refresh and deepen her own inspiration. For final pronouncements men did not look to the schools of the frontier countries and daughter churches.

Now there are to be found in Behar, the ancient Magadha, to this day, the vestiges of a long history of Buddhist sculpture in many phases and developments. No one has ever denied to India the pre-Buddhistic existence of secular sculpture of the human form. In front of the chaitya at Karli (date 129 B.C.) we find integral figures of men and women which may be portraits of kings and queens, or of donors and their wives. In the Rail of Bharhut we find figures in the round, and abundance of animal representation. And the whole range of Naga-types is common from the earliest times.

No one has ever pretended that these sculptures

were foreign in origin. In fact competent critics are wont to turn to them for the exemplification of the somewhat vague entity that may be called the indigenous impulse in Indian art. In the low carvings in relief, therefore, on the Asokan Rail at Bodh-Gaya, we are not called upon to suspect a foreign origin. We may take these frankly as we find them, as examples of the Indian art of the year 250 B.C. or thereabouts. From this point on we watch the development of Buddhistic art in Behar. Here we have the enclosure built about the sacred tree. Again we have a footprint, as at Gaya itself, where that now worshipped as the Vishnupada was almost certainly originally a Buddhistic symbol. Behar was at one time full of stupas, but the very fact that these have been defaced and treated as mounds or hills is testimony to the fact that they were probably as plain in the time of Asoka as that now at Sarnath or at Sanchi. It is true enough that at its birth Buddhism found all holiness in that plain dome-shaped cairn of earth and bricks, which sometimes did, as at Rajgir, and sometimes did not, as at Sanchi, conceal a deposit of relics. Amongst the small votive stupas which it became the fashion for pilgrims and visitors to leave at sacred shrines, there are many of this phase of development.

It was essential that they should have five parts, clearly distinguishable, and a system of philosophy grew up which connected these with the five elements—earth, air, fire, water, and ether.

BUDDHA'S LOTUS THRONE SUPPORTED BY NÂGAS
(Kenheri Caves)

It must have been soon after Asoka that attempts were made to evolve a portrait-statue of Buddha. In accordance with the Indian character as well as with the severe truthfulness of early Hinayana doctrines, the first efforts in this direction would almost certainly be intensely realistic. They would be filled with a striving after literal fact. In far-away Sanchi, even as late as 150 B.C., we have the bas-reliefs on the great gateways representing anything and everything Buddhistic that could be worshipped save and except Buddha himself. But this is only what we might expect if, as we have supposed, precedence in this matter really belonged to Magadha. At some later date we find at Kenheri illustrations of the blending of the old school of art to which Sanchi belonged—in which a story was told, in picture form—and this new idea of the supernatural personage appearing as heroic amongst even the holiest of mortal men. This particular panel illustrates the Jatakas (birth-stories), which must have been the absorbing literature and romance of early Buddhism, and were in themselves only a hint of the place which the personality of its founder must sooner or later assume in the religion. This figure of a former Buddha is not naked, as might be supposed. It is merely clothed in muslin so fine as to be almost invisible. Grünwedel gives a reproduction of a clay seal from Bodh-Gaya, in which we have another specimen of this same period in the idealisation of the Buddha. The little turret-like patterns which accompany it are stupas. But the Buddha himself is imaged in front of a temple-stupa.

To this period probably belongs the story that when Ajatasatru wished for a portrait of the Teacher, he allowed his shadow to fall on a piece of cloth, and then the outline was filled in with colour. Grünwedel suggests that this story shows a desire to claim canonical authority for the portrait-statue. Whether this be so or not, it certainly does indicate incidentally that the Buddhist world itself ascribed the origin of the Master's image to Magadha. The supreme example of this school of sculpture is undoubtedly the Great Buddha of Nalanda, which is to this day the pride of the country-folk at Baragaon, who call it Mahadev. To the same school belongs also the Buddha of the temple at Bodh-Gaya. And we cannot do better than take as an example of the type the Buddha from Anuradhapura in Ceylon.

These are true statues, not mere bas-reliefs. And perhaps the great proof of their early occurrence in the Buddhist series lies precisely here, that they were found in Ceylon, where the enthusiasm of Indian intercourse was a marked feature of the age immediately succeeding Asoka, and where the Hinayana theology would not be friendly to statuary like the images characteristic of a rich mythology.

The clay seal is of extraordinary interest. The Buddha himself appears to be seated in something like the temple of Bodh-Gaya, with branches of the sacred tree appearing behind and above.

OLD INDIAN CLAY SEAL FROM BODH-GAYA

Original in the Berlin Museum

The plain stupas all round show the contemporary development of that symbol. Now there was a moment when, by the simultaneous modification of all its five parts, the stupa was transformed into something very like what we now recognise as a temple. Specimens of this phase abound in the neighbourhood of Nalanda, and indeed some hand has gathered a quantity of representative examples together and placed them on the bathing *ghât* at Baragaon. Except in the instances of this clay seal figured by Grünwedel and a stupa which is to be seen in the Sonar Bhandar Cave at Rajgir, however, I do not remember ever to have seen this phase of the stupa associated with an image. The panelled example at Rajgir would seem to be old because of the stiffness with which the standing Buddha is portrayed. He stands with feet apart, as in the drawings of children. But never have I seen a work of art which was equal to this in the depth and strength of the personal conviction which it found means to convey. The Buddha is clad in the usual invisible clothing of the period. He is stiffly and awkwardly posed, and conveys the idea of gigantic size. Outside the sunken panel on which he is carved, above him and to right and left, appear branches of trees of recognisable species, and each such branch half conceals a hand with pointing finger. The whole effect is extraordinary. The words "This is the man!" are almost to be heard. This vividness of feeling combined with the stiffness of the work would incline one to place the statue early, and with this the evidence of the clay seal now before us is in agreement. But if we are to assign an early date to sculpture of this description, we must completely abandon the notion of pre-Buddhistic Indian art as semi-barbarous and crude. This degree of expressive power and this irresistible impulse towards the rapid modification of fixed symbols argues a long familiarity with the tools and the method of plastic enunciation. The Hinayana doctrine would incline the stupa-maker at first to its aniconic development, but the innate genius of the Indian race for man-worship and its fundamental fearlessness of symbolism would triumph in the end over all the artificial barriers of theology, and the aniconic stupa would inevitably receive its icon. Of this moment our clay seal is a memorial.

The next step was to take the unmodified stupa, and carve on it four small Buddhas, one on each of its sides. We can well understand the impulse that led to this. The dagoba was a geographical point, from which Buddha himself shone forth to north, south, east, and west upon the world. It is the same idea which in a later age led to the colossal images of the Roshana Buddha in Japan. The very thought of the Master, with his spiritual empire in the foreign missions, brought up a geographical conception. And this geographical idea it is that finds expression in those small and simple stupas, carved each with the four Buddhas, which one could often hold on the palm of one hand. In imitation of these, but much later, four Buddhas were placed round the great stupa at Sanchi.

These points established, the course of history is clear enough. He who would understand the development of Buddhist art has only to follow the development of the stupa. This is as fixed in its succession of forms as a chronological scale. At first it is plain, as at Sanchi. Then it is ornamented with the Asokan rail itself, which by this time shares the general sanctity of association, as at Karli, Bhaja, Kenheri, and Ajanta, Caves Nine and Ten. Then it is elongated, and forms what we regard as a temple. Then the small stupa takes to itself the four Buddhas. Gradually these undergo changes. The line of development hesitates for awhile, and then branches off in a new direction. The four figures become four heads, but whether of Brahma or the Mother of the Universe is not yet determined. Gradually the name of the Great God is triumphant, the pillar-like top in the middle of the four heads is more and more emphasized, and along this line of development the stupa is finally converted into the Shiva emblem of Hinduism. One of the worship-mantras to this day ascribes to Shiva the possession of five faces. That is to say, his emblem is still to the eye of faith a dome-shaped projection in the midst of four heads.

At that moment when the four seated Buddhas were becoming the four heads, the image of Buddha was being detached from the stupa altogether, and entering on a new phase of development as an icon or symbol of the highest sanctity. It was because this was happening that the stupa itself had been enabled to undergo the changes necessary to convert it into the Shiva. It is now, then, that we may place the evolution of the image of the First Sermon at Benares. This was not so fixed as is commonly supposed. In the caves of the second period at Ajanta—Seven, Eleven, Fifteen, Sixteen, and Seventeen—we may judge for ourselves of the rigour or latitude of the convention. No two of these are exactly alike. Seven is one of the earliest, because the ambulatory which was essential to the chaitya-dagoba is here found, at immense cost of labour, to have been provided for the image in the shrine also, showing that the excavators were as yet inexperienced in the different uses of the two. The shrine, or *gandalcuti*, was not yet stereotyped into a mere hall of perfumes, or incense, as Hiouen Tsang calls it. This processional use of the shrine explains the elaborate carving of the side-walls here, to be described later. In the image, which is still more or less intact at Sarnath itself, we find an effeminacy of treatment which is very startling. The predella too is unexpected, holding worshipping figures turning the wheel of the law, instead of the peaceful animals lying quietly side by side in that wondrous eventide. Grünwedel points out that the use of the halo speaks of the existence of an old school of art in the country. So also do the flying *devas* and the wheel and the symbolistic animals. The artist was speaking a language already understood by the people. The first images had arisen out of the desire to express to foreign peoples something of the ideal in the form of the beloved personality. This particular image now became pre-eminent as a mark of the fact that viharas were becoming colleges. Buddhism was taking upon itself the task of national education and scholarship.

But the original idea, in its original home, had not ceased to develop. There was always the irresistible instinct to express the growing and changing forms of the national faith in plastic concreteness. The evolution of Shiva and Saivism, being first to branch off from the original Hinayana stream, early hardened down, as far as Behar was concerned, into the use as its supreme expression of an emblem, instead of an image. It gave rise to a certain amount of descriptive sculpture, as in the case of Kartikeyya, for instance, but it did not share to the full in the later artistic and sculptural impulse. Still there remained unregimented the old idea of the Mother or Adisakti, and sculptural allusions to this begin to be frequent in the later phases of Buddhist art, along with that which supersedes everything under the Gupta emperors as the religion of the state. Here we come upon a wholly new symbolism, that of Narayan or Vishnu, the Great God of those who worship Krishna. Artistically speaking, indeed, on the west side of India, it took centuries to exhaust the sculptural impetus associated with Shiva, and much history is written in the fact. He rose upon the horizon as the third member of a trinity—reflecting the Buddhist trinity, of Buddha, Dharma, Sanga—a conception which is recorded in the large cave at Elephanta. At Ellora and at Elephanta he is almost passionately revered, so absorbing is his hold on the artistic imagination, and such is the wealth of illustration that they lavish on him. In Magadha, however, creative art is playing with two different ideas at this time. They are the Mother—later to become the occasion of an alliance between Brahmanistic and Mongolian ideas—and Vishnu or Narayana. At Ayodhya, indeed, the second member of the Trinity had already given rise to a humanised reflection of Buddha in the notion of a human incarnation, which had been preached as a gospel in the Ramayana. The poet Kalidas had written the romance of both branches of Hinduism in his *Kumara Sambhava* and *Raghuvamsa.* And throughout all the works of this period the attempt is constantly made to prove the identity of Rama with Shiva. This is satisfactory evidence that the worship of Shiva was elaborated as a system earlier than that of Vishnu or his incarnations. It also shows the intense grasp which the Indian philosophy of unity had gained over the national mind. The stupa continued even now to reflect the changing phases of thought. Hence it is doubtless to this time that we may ascribe those Shiva-lingams covered with the feet of the Lord that are to be met with occasionally in Rajgir.

After Shiva, however, the attention of sculptors in Magadha was more and more concentrated on the image of Narayana. It is probably an error to think of this as rigidly fixed in form. An unyielding convention is always the end of an evolution, never the beginning. And like Shiva in the west, so also Narayana in Magadha is connected with Buddha by a long series of gradual modifications. Sometimes we can detect Chinese influence in a particular statue. With the rise of the Guptas and the necessity of a gold coinage, it would seem as if Chinese minters had been employed, just as in his time and capital Kanishka had undoubtedly employed Greeks for the same purpose. There is no difficulty in imagining that such Chinese workmen might sometimes be employed on a statue. The fact that the form itself, however, was not of their initiating is best proved by the gradual transitions which connect it with the image of Buddha. So much has been said, so lightly, about the impossibility of Indian inventiveness, that it is necessary to guard from time to time against petty misconception. Another point of the same kind arises with regard to Hinduism itself. It may be well to say that Buddhism did not originate the ideas which in their totality make up Hinduism. Indeed Buddhism was itself the result of those ideas. But by its immense force of organisation, it achieved such a unification of the country and the people, that it forced upon the Brahmans the *organisation* of Hinduism.

The conception of Narayana was taken up by the Guptas to be made into the basis of a national faith. This took shape as Krishna, and its epic was written in the Mahabharata. But the image associated with it was still that of Narayana. This was the form that was carried to the south by the missionary travellers who were the outcome of the educational and propagandist zeal of the Guptas, and there it is worshipped to this day. It was an image of this type that was placed by Skanda Gupta on the top of the Bhitari Lat when he erected it in A.D. 455 for the purpose of recording on his father's *sradh* pillar his own victory over the Huns.

There is therefore a continuous history of sculpture in Behar, beginning with the earliest period of Buddhism, and passing gradually, and by easily distinguished phases, into various forms of modern Hinduism. In this continuous development we can distinguish local schools, and this is the best answer to those who would talk of foreign influence.

The comparatively coarse, artisan-like work of Bodh-Gaya can never be mistaken for the soft, exquisitely curved and moulded forms of Baragaon, the ancient Nalanda. The Hindu carvings of Rajgir, again, are distinct from both. It is almost impossible therefore to speak of a single Magadhan school of sculpture. Much of the Rajgir work is Saivite in subject, being earlier than the Narayana types of Baragaon.

Early Buddhism has thus had two products: the portrait-statue and the iconic stupa. The stupa in its turn has given birth to the Shiva emblem and to the image proper. The image has developed itself as Buddha, and also borne as an offshoot the image of Narayana. But with this extraordinary energy of modification, only to be credited when we remember the wonderful theological and philosophical fertility of the Indian mind, it is not to be supposed that the stupa as such had ceased to develop. There was at least one well-marked phase before it yet. The world, for the monk, was peopled with meditating figures. The church was ideally a great host who had attained through the Master's might. The lotus on which he sat enthroned had many branches. This thought also found expression in the stupa. The same idea is laboriously sculptured on the walls of the shrine in Ajanta Seven. And on reaching more distant parts of the order, no doubt it was this development that gave rise to the multiplication of small meditating figures and their being placed even on straight lines, or amongst leafage, wherever the architecture gave the slightest opportunity or excuse.

All this goes to show that Magadha remained (as she began), throughout the Buddhist age the source and creative centre, alike for theology and for the system of symbolism which was instrumental in carrying that theology far and wide. Waddell some years ago communicated a paper to the Royal Asiatic Society in which he urged that the original types of the Mahayanist images of Tibet must be sought for in Magadha. He was undoubtedly right, and the conclusion is forced upon us that the doctrine of the Bodhisattvas must have been born in Magadha, and from there have been poured out upon the Council of Kanishka, at Taxila, or Jalandhara, or Kandahar. The Kanishkan Council thus would only give effect to the opinions and speculations that had long been gathering in the eastern centre. The doctrine of the Bodhisattvas came fullblown to Jalandhara and there gathered the force that carried it over the Chinese Empire. Indeed the very fact that the commentaries of this Council were written down in Sanskrit is strong presumptive evidence for the vitality and force of the eastern elements at the Council, an added witness to the prestige which their presence conferred upon it. This Council is said to have sat some months, and we are expressly told that its work lay in reconciling and giving the stamp of orthodoxy to all the eighteen schools of Buddhism which by that time had come into existence. That is to say, it did not professs to give currency to new doctrines. It merely conferred the seal of its authority on phases of the faith which would otherwise have tended to be mutually exclusive. This in itself is evidence of the way in which its members were saturated with the characteristic eastern idea of Vedantic toleration. And Buddhism stands in this Council alone in religious history as an example of the union of the powers of organisation and discretion with those of theological fervour and devotional conviction in the highest degree. Evidently we have here a great body of monk-pundits, imported for the summer into Gandhara. Probably many of them never returned to their mother-communities, but remained, to form the basis of that great monastic development which Gandhara was afterwards to see.

The priority of Magadha requires little further argument. At the time of the Council the synthesis of the Mahayana was already more or less complete. And in accordance with this is the fact that on the recently-discovered relic casket of Kanishka are three figures, Buddha and two Bodhisattvas. In harmony with this is the further fact that the few inscriptions hitherto discovered in the Gandhara country are all dated between A.D. 57 and 328. We can see that after the evolution of the ornate and over-multiplied style of Gandhara Buddhism could not have had the energy to begin over again in India to build up a new art with its slow and sincere history of a growing symbolism. As a matter of fact, Gandhara was in the full tide of her artistic success in the fourth and early fifth century, when Magadha had already reached the stage of pre-occupation with images of Narayana.

Thus a definite theory has been enunciated of the chronological succession of religious ideas in Indian sculpture. According to this theory, Magadha was the source and centre of the Indian unity, both philosophically and artistically. This province was, in fact, like the heart of an organism whose systole and diastole are felt to its remotest bounds with a certain rhythmic regularity of pulsation, as tides of thought and inspiration. All such will not be felt equally in all directions. In this case the work in Ceylon was the result of an early impulse, Gandhara much later, and possibly we should find, if this were the place to follow up the question, that Tibet was evangelised as the fruit of a still later pulsation of the central energy. This being so, the fact would stand proved that Gandhara was a disciple and not a guru in the matter of religious symbolism. The question is, Can this relationship be demonstrated, and how?

A crucial test would be afforded if we could find anything in the art of Gandhara itself which might show it to be a derived style. Creative works, like myths, almost always include some unconscious sign-manual of their origin and relations. What they deliberately state may be untrue, or, as in the present case perhaps, may be misunderstood. But what they mention is usually eloquent, to patient eyes, of the actual fact. It has already been pointed out by Mr. E. B. Havell, in his *Indian Sculpture and Painting*, that even the Buddha-types, the serious affirmations of Gandharan art, could not possibly be mistaken for originals. And if anyone will take the trouble to go into the hall of the Calcutta Museum and look for himself, it is difficult to see how this argument can be answered. Who that has steeped himself in the eastern conception of the Buddha—unbroken calm, immeasurable detachment, and a vastness as of eternity—can take the smart, military-looking young men there displayed, with their moustaches carefully trimmed to the utmost point of nicety, and their perfect actuality and worldliness of expression, as satisfying presentments? In very sooth do these Gandharan Buddhas, as Mr. Havell says, bear their derivative character plainly stamped upon their faces.

But it may be held that this is the end of the argument, not the beginning. There may be many incapable of appraising an expression, who will want more elementary and incontrovertible grounds of judgment, and for these we have plenty of evidence.

The first discovery of the Gandharan monasteries, with their treasures of sculpture, in 1848 and 1852, seemed to the minds of European scholars, naturally enough, an event of the greatest artistic and historic importance; and Fergusson has left on record, in his invaluable book, an account of that impression, and also of its grounds, in a form which will never be repeated. Unfortunately the finds were very carelessly and incompetently dealt with, and their mutual relations and story thus rendered irrecoverable. Out of the eight or ten sites which have been examined, however, it is possible to say that Jamalgarhi and Takht-i-Bahi are probably the most modern, while Shah-Dheri was very likely the most ancient. Judging by the plans and description which Fergusson gives, indeed, of this last-named monastery, it would seem to have belonged to the same age and phase of Buddhism as the old disused Cave Number One at Elephanta —a long verandah-like chaitya cave which evidently held a circular dagoba on a square altar. The sculptures as well as the plans of the later monasteries, according to Fergusson, appear to be characterised by excessive duplication. The architecture associated with them seems to have been extraordinarily mixed and unrestrained in character. Amongst the leafage of pillar-capitals occur hundreds of little Buddhas. But it would have been obvious that these were late examples, even if Fergusson had not already announced that opinion. The main chamber of each monastery seems to have been a hall or court, either square or circular, in the middle of which stood an altar surmounted by a dagoba. Round this the walls were broken up into quantities of small niches or chapels, each one containing its image, and the whole decorated to excess. Regarding this as representing theoretically the vihara surrounding a dagoba of earlier days, Fergusson is very properly struck with astonishment by the phenomenon. In no Buddhist monument in India of which he knows, he says, have the monks ever been thrust out of the cells to make way for images. If he had not been told what the plans were and where they came from, he would unhesitatingly have pronounced them to be from Jain monasteries of the ninth and tenth centuries. From architectural considerations he thinks that the classical influences seen here must have culminated at and after the

RELIEF FROM MUHAMMAD NARI, IN YUSUFZAI

time of Constantine, that is from A.D. 306 onwards, and that they speak even more loudly of Byzantium than of Rome. He has difficulty in understanding how Byzantium should make itself so strongly felt in a remote province, without leaving any trace on the arts of intermediate kingdoms, such as the Sassanian empire. But we have already seen that this is no real difficulty, since it is precisely at their terminal points that those influences act, which pour along the world's great trade-routes. The Indian man of genius in modern times makes his personality felt in London, and not in France, though he landed at Marseilles.

For ourselves, however, while we grant the mixture of elements in Gandhara, the question arises whether the latter did not influence Byzantium quite as much as the Western capital influenced it. According to the data thus propounded, we may expect to find amongst these Gandharan sculptures a vast mixture of decorative elements, all subordinated to the main intention of setting forth in forms of eternal beauty and lucidity the personality of Buddha, it being understood that the form of the Buddha himself is taken more or less unchanged from the artistic traditions of Magadha. It may be well to take as our first point for examination the Gandharan use of the Asokan rail. We are familiar with the sanctity of this rail as a piece of symbolism in the early ages of Buddhism. At Sanchi—undoubtedly a very close spiritual province of Magadha, and intimately knit to Sarnath in particular—we find it used not only pictorially, but also to bound and divide spaces. As we have seen, the gradual forgetting of the meaning of architectural features like the Asokan rail and the horse-shoe ornament affords a very good scale of chronology by which to date Indian monuments. Nowhere have we a better instance of this than in the Gandharan use of the rail. In the relief from Muhammad Nari we have several stages in its gradual forgetting, ending with its becoming a mere chequer, as at the top of the lower panel. This illustration is extraordinarily valuable for us, moreover, for the way in which the figure of the Buddha is violently inserted amongst strikingly incongruous surroundings. We can almost see the two opposing traditions, by the discord between him with his clothes of the eastern provinces and attitude which forbids activity, and his environment. This Buddha is not, however, a very successful example of the tradition out of which he comes. He has a singularly uneasy and intruded look on the height where he is seen uncomfortably perched.

A second feature that will strike the observant in this picture is the curious use of the lotus-throne. It looks as if the sculptor had been told to seat his subject on a lotus, but had had a very vague idea of how this should be done. We can almost hear those verbal instructions which he has tried to carry out. In the Buddha from Loriyan Tangai is another instance of a similar difficulty. The sculptor in this second fragment, rightly feeling that the seat, as he understood the order, could not possibly support the hero, has adopted the ingenious device of introducing two worshipping figures to support the knees! Still more noticeable, however, are the two feet, or petals reversed, which he has adopted to make of the lotus-throne a lotus-bearing tripod. With this we may compare the genuine Indian treatment of a lotus-throne from Nepal. At the same time, the early age of the lotus-petal ornament is seen on an Asokan doorway in the vihara at Sanchi, the only doorway that has escaped improvement at a later age. Another curious example of the attempt to render symbolistic scenes, according to a verbal or literary description of them, is seen in the picture representing the familiar First Sermon, at Benares. There is undoubted power of composition here. To the untrained European eye these beauties may make it more appealing than the old Sarnath images of the shrine type at Ajanta. Still, the fact remains of an obvious effort to render to order an idea and a convention only half understood. And the place occupied by the *dharma-chakra* is like a signature appended to the confession of this struggle. It will be noted too, that this *dharma-chakra* is wrong. The *trisul* should have pointed away from the *chakra*. Other curious and interesting examples of the same kind may be seen in the Museum.

Grünwedel has drawn attention to the question of clothing, but apparently without understanding the full significance of the facts. It will be noticed throughout these illustrations that the artists tend to clothe Buddha in the dress that would be appropriate in a cold climate. Our illustration of the relief found at Muhammed Nari is in this respect specially valuable. It is probably early Gandharan, since the attempt to render the clothes of Buddha and the ornaments of the women correctly is very evident, and, it may be added, extremely unsuccessful. It would appear as if this relief had been commissioned by some monk who was a native of Magadha. But no Magadhan workman would have draped the muslin in such a fashion at the knees or on the arm. Yet the correct intention is manifest from the bare right shoulder. Afterwards Gandharan artists solved this problem by evolving a style of costume of their own for the sacred figures. As this was their own, they were much happier in rendering it. But another point that jars on the Indian eye is the allusion here made to women's jewellery. The matter has been mentioned as needing particular care—that we can see. But the results are forced and inappropriate, and serve only to emphasize their own failure. Instances of the particular facts abound. It is unnecessary to enter further into detail.

Throughout these illustrations what may be called the architectural ornament is very noticeable. It has no connection whatever with what we are accustomed to think of as characteristically Buddhist. The spacings are constantly made with the stem of the date-palm, and ends and borders are painfully modish and secular. Such a want of ecclesiastical feeling, in sculpture that aims at a devotional use, can probably not be paralleled at any other age or place. The Corinthian finials and floral ornaments, to eyes looking for the gravity and significance of old Asiatic decoration, are very irritating. An excellent example is the Loriyan Tangai Buddha. Here we have a singularly phonetic piece of statuary. The feeling it portrays is exquisite. The pious beasts with their paws crossed are not less beautiful than the peacock which stands with tail spread to proclaim to the world the glories of the dawn of the morning of Nirvana. Yet even here a jarring note is struck in the irrelevancy of the borders, like a piece of school-girl embroidery.

Gandhara did really, however, have its period of influence over the sculpture of India. But this period began when its own style had reached its zenith. Comparatively early in the sixth century incursions of Huns swept over the country, and, in a year to which the date of A.D. 540 has been assigned, we are expressly told of the destruction of monasteries and stupas in an outburst of vengeful cruelty, by the tyrant Mihiragula. This destruction was not complete, for a hundred years later the pilgrim Hiouen Tsang passed through the country and found many monasteries in full vigour. Still, it cannot have failed to drive large numbers of the Gandharan monks to take refuge in the viharas and monastic universities of India. This is the event that is marked in the Ajantan series of caves by Number Nineteen. Here on the outside we have for the first time the employment of carvings of Buddha as part of the decorations included in the original architectural scheme. It is a secularised Buddha, moreover ; a Buddha who, as already said, has been seen from a new point of view as a great historical character. He receives a banner. He is crowned by flying figures. The chequer-pattern appears here and there, in lieu of the Asokan rail which it represents. And inside the hall we have that great multitude of Buddhas, in the triforium and on the capitals, in those richly-decorated niches, for which Fergusson's account of the Gandharan monasteries has prepared us. But these represent a more Indianised and religious type than the panels of the outside. The date and source of the new influence is still further fixed by the indubitable fact of the *choga*, or robe, worn by the Buddha on the dagoba.

We have seen that, according to the evidence of the inscription, Cave Seventeen with its shrine, and the cistern under Eighteen, may be taken as completed about the year A.D. 520. It is my personal opinion that the right-hand series of caves from Six to One were undertaken, or at least finished, not long after this date, and distinctly before the arrival of the refugees from Gandhara. Ajanta must have been one of the most notable of Indian universities, and the influence of the north-west upon its art does not cease with Nineteen. The whole interior surface of Twenty-six—probably undertaken by the abbot Buddha Bhadra at some date subsequent to the visit of Hiouen Tsang in the middle of the seventh century—is covered with carvings, culminating in an immense treatment of the subject so much beloved by the latest Gandharan sculptors, the Mahanirvana of Buddha. The Buddha in this carving is 23 feet long, and even the curious tripod which seems to support the beggar's bowl and crutch is reproduced. This duplication of a known subject is very eloquent.

We may conclude, then, that a vital artistic intercourse was now maintained between Gandhara and Ajanta, and in this connection the carved ornament of palm-leaves, so reminiscent of the bole of the date-palm, amongst the ornaments of the doorway on Cave Twenty-three, is of the utmost significance.

But a second catastrophe occurred in Gandhara, and the destruction of the monastic foundations in that country was complete. The wars between the Saracenic Mohammedans and the Chinese Empire culminated about the middle of the eighth century in the utter defeat and expulsion of the Eastern power (A.D. 751). The Arabs must then have swept Gandhara from end to end, and every monk who had not fled was doubtless put to the sword. India was the obvious refuge of the consequent crowd of *émigrés*, and art and education the only means open to them of repaying the hospitality of the Indian monasteries and governments. From this period must date the small panelled Buddhas which have been carved all over the older caves, not only at Ajanta, but also at Kenheri, at Karli, and doubtless elsewhere. The great durbar hall at Kenheri (Cave 10) is filled with a splendidly planned and coherent scheme of such decoration. But the artists have not always been so considerate. They have begun their carvings in the midst of older work, and side by side with it—probably wherever they were not stopped by the presence of paintings—without the slightest regard to the appropriateness of the combination. For some years the face of the rock must have swarmed with these industrious sculptors working all at the same time. And then some other political catastrophe stopped all chisels in a moment. The cheerful hum of study and ringing of tools on the stone were suddenly silenced. The caves were swept bare alike of the monks and their students; and though not destroyed, Ajanta lay for centuries deserted, like the Gandharan monasteries before it.

But some of the Gandharan exiles had taken up the task of general education, and it is probably from the period of the Arab conquest of Gandhara in A.D. 751 that we must date the Brahmanical organisation of learning, reflecting the monastic universities of the Buddhists, in *tolls* and *akaras*, together with the widespread diffusion of the Saka or Scythic era, dating from 57 B.C.—in all parts of Northern India. Thus a remote province repaid its debt to the Magadhan and Indian Mother-land.

When we come to consider their relative dates, the influence of Gandhara on European art through Byzantium is hardly a matter that will be seriously denied. Anyone who looks at a scene in the Lumbini Garden, which is exhibited in the Calcutta Museum, not to mention many of the illustrations in Grünwedel's book, must acknowledge the debt owed to Gandhara by Christian art from the end of the fourth century and onwards. To some of us in Europe to this day, just as the Gregorian is the most devotional of all music, so even the art of Catholicism only seems fully religious in proportion as it returns upon the stiffness and gravity of that early Byzantine which is so obviously the product of the union of Eastern and Western elements in Gandhara.

For the art of Gandhara made a wonderful attempt at blending the epic feeling of European classical art with Eastern wealth of decoration. Such minglings can never be attempted artificially or of set purpose. They cannot be reached because we should like to reach them. They have to be unconscious, organic, a matter of growth round some idea in which the whole heart is engaged. Aristotle lamented the fall of Greek art from *epos* to *pathos*, from heroic dignity to human emotion. But even *pathos* could be made heroic, as the East well knew, by consecration to an ideal; and that ideal the Gandharan artists found in Buddha.

There Eastern and Western alike fell under the eastern spell. The thought of a human being who was at the same time incarnate Godhead fascinated them. Influenced by the tendency of classical Europe to exalt the human and virile side of every concept, they busied themselves in portraying the companions and disciples of Buddha. These became as essential a part of the scheme of the evangel as the Master himself. The old Asiatic conception of a story told in a series of bas-reliefs, as we see it at Sanchi, came to their aid, and we have a singularly impressive *epos* of the ideal rendered into stone. Apostolic processions and saintly choirs, as we know them from the fourth century onwards in Christian art, whether Byzantine, Roman, or Gothic, began in the Gandharan art of the second and third. There, from Buddhist monks trying to instruct their workmen in the feeling and artistic traditions of Magadha, was learnt the power to utter the divine epic whose hero was the conqueror of the mind, perfect in chastity as in compassion, and its appeal to man in the name neither of country nor state, nor yet in that of personal emotion, but in something which is beyond either and includes both, the passion of the upward-striving soul.

We cannot too clearly understand that while Gandharan art made no contribution whatever to the Indian ideal of Buddhahood, while it created nothing that could stand a moment's comparison with the work of the nameless artist of Nalanda, it nevertheless captured Buddha, and through his life and his disciples elaborated a religious type for the West. From the moment when Constantine established his new capital at the ancient site on the shores of the Bosphorus, that is to say, from about A.D. 335, the influence of the East on the art of the younger faith would become as energetic as the sculptural capacities of the artisans of Byzantium had already shown themselves in the Gandharan monasteries.

Magadha has produced symbols whose dignity Gandhara was never able to approach. But in complex composition, in power of architectural story-telling, in dignity of the decorative synthesis, it is difficult to feel that the ultimate achievements of Gandhara and her posterity had ever before been approached, even at Sanchi.

It must never be supposed, however, that Gandhara was Europe. In spite of the Western elements, whose existence its art demonstrates, Gandhara was pre-eminently Asiatic. And never again perhaps will the actual facts be better or more comprehensively stated than in the memorable words of Havell, in his *Indian Sculpture and Painting*:—

"Indian idealism during the greater part of this time was the dominating note in the art of Asia which was thus brought into Europe; and when we find a perfectly oriental atmosphere and strange echoes of Eastern symbolism in the mediæval cathedrals of Europe, and see their structural growth gradually blossoming with all the exuberance of Eastern imagery, it is impossible to avoid the conclusion that Gothic architecture and Gothic handicraft owe very much to the absorption by the *bauhutten* of Germany, and other Western craft-guilds, of Asiatic art and science, brought by the thousands of Asiatic craftsmen who entered Europe in the first millennium of the Christian era, a period which in the minds of Europeans is generally a blank, because the 'Great Powers' were then located in Asia instead of in Europe. Byzantine art and Gothic art derived their inspiration from the same source—the impact of Asiatic thought upon the civilisation of the Roman Empire. The first shows its effect upon the art of the Greek and Latin races, the other its influence upon the Romanesque art of Teutonic and Celtic races. The spirit of Indian idealism breathes in the mosaics of St. Mark's at Venice, just as it shines in the mystic splendours of the Gothic cathedrals; through the delicate tracery of their jewelled windows, filled with the stories of saints and martyrs; in all their richly sculptured arches, fairy vaulting and soaring pinnacles and spires. The Italian Renaissance marks the reversion of Christian art to the pagan ideals of Greece, and the capture of art by the bookmen, leading to our present dilettantism and archæological views of art."

The Indian San Marco

There is outside Florence a Dominican monastery which is famous for the fact that once upon a time Fra Giovanni of Fiesole [1]—better known as Fra

[1] Fra Giovanni of Fiesole lived from A.D. 1387 to 1455.

Angelico—lived within its walls and covered them with his saints and angels against the gilded background of heaven. Later, it was the one undecorated chamber in this monastery that Savonarola took as his own, when he came as a Dominican to San Marco. The old convent remains to this day for Europe one of the trysting-places of righteousness and beauty. We know not which are more real, the angels that still blaze upon the walls, or the lives that once were lived within them.

Something of the same feeling must have clung to Ajanta in the late fifth to the eighth centuries. A great art-tradition had grown up about its name. It is very likely, of course, that such a tradition was commoner in the India of those days than we can now realise. Perhaps many buildings were covered within with emblazoned literature. Gold and scarlet and blue were often, it may be, united together, to sing the heroic dreams of the time to the eyes of all. But it is difficult to imagine that in any country the splendours of Ajanta could seem ordinary. Those wonderful arches and long colonnades stretching along the face of the hillside, with the blue eaves of slate-coloured rock overhanging them, and the knowledge of glowing beauty covering every inch of the walls behind them—no array of colleges or cathedrals in the whole world could make such a thing seem ordinary. For it was doubtless as colleges that the great task was carried out in them, and we can see that it took centuries. That is to say, for some hundreds of years Ajanta was thought of in India as one of the great opportunities of the artist, or maybe as a grand visual exposition of the monkish classics.

We can judge of the length of time over which the work spread, the time during which the tradition was growing up, by the fact that the paintings in Cave Sixteen, which is older, are stiffer and more purely decorative, such of them as remain, than those in Seventeen. But even those of Sixteen are not the oldest pictures at Ajanta. When we enter Cave Nine for the first time, we find ourselves in the company of a great host of rapt and adoring worshippers. They stand on every face of the simple octagonal pillars, with their looks turned always to the solemn looking stupa or dagoba. They have each one of them a nimbus behind him. They might be Bodhisattvas, but the feeling of worship so fills the little chapel that instinctively one puts them down as the early saints and companions of Buddha, and turns with a feeling of awe to join their adoration of the dome-like altar. They are not archaic in the sense of crudity. But they have the feeling of an early world about them. They are like the work of Fra Angelico, but may be anything in date from the second century onwards, that is to say a thousand years before his time! In the aisle that runs behind the pillars the walls are covered with simple scenes from the Teaching of Buddha. Here we find the mother bringing her dead son, and the Master seated with his disciples about him. But

VERANDA, CAVE NUMBER SEVENTEEN, AJANTA

we return to the nave, and, again looking at the forms on the pillar-faces, let ourselves dream for a moment, till we seem to hear the deep *Adoramus* with which they fill the air around us.

This silent throng of painted worshippers suggests to the mind's eye the worship itself that once filled the little cathedral chapel. We see the procession of monks that must have entered at one door, made *pradakshina* about the altar, and gone out on the other side. We see the lights that they carried, the incense they waved, the prostrations they made, and the silent congregation of lay-folk and students who may have looked on them from the back of the nave, as even now at a Hindu *arati* one may kneel apart and watch. We hear the chanting of the monks as the incense was swung, and we realise the problem that Buddhism had to solve in giving solemnity and impressiveness to a worship denuded of the splendours and significance of sacrifice. It must have been this consciousness that led to the rapid organisation of a ritual whose elements were all indeed derived from the Vedic, but which was in its entirety the most characteristic and organic expression of democratie religion that the world had ever seen. The history of Christian worship has not yet been written, but it is open to us to believe that when it is, its debt to the chaityas will be found greater than is now suspected.

The host of saints and apostles brings us face to face with another thought. We see how much the stupa-shaped altar meant to the Buddhist worshipper. We begin to feel our way back to all that it implied. Sanctified by ages of consecration —for there was a pre-Buddhistic stupa-worship; Newgrange, the Irish Sanchi, is a thousand years older than Buddha—men saw in that domed mound more than we now can ever fathom. Yet we may look at it and try to summon up all that we have felt for this symbol or for that. How curious are the things to which the heart of man has gone out in its fulness from time to time! A couple of spars lashed together at right angles; a couple of crescent-shaped axes back to back; a cairn. And each of these has had the power in its day to make men die joyfully and merrily as a piece of good fortune! Usually it is easier to imagine this when the emblem has taken to itself an icon or image. The crucifix might better make martyrs than the cross, one thinks. The stupa with the Buddha upon it stirs one deeper than the stupa or dagoba alone. Yet here amongst the choir of saints we catch a hint of quite another feeling, and we understand that when the icon was added to the emblem faith was already dim.

The University of Ajanta departs in its paintings from primitive simplicity. Cave Sixteen is highly decorated, and Cave Seventeen a veritable labyrinth of beauty and narrative. Everywhere flames out some mighty subject, and everywhere are connecting links and ornamental figures. Not once does inspiration fail, though the soft brightness to-day

AJANTA: INTERIOR OF CAVE NUMBER TWENTY-SIX

COMPARTMENT FROM THE THIRD ARCHWAY OF THE EAST GATEWAY AT SANCHI

is for the most part dim, and the colours have largely to be guessed at. What are the subjects? Ah, that is the question! Here at any rate is one rendered specially famous, for the moment, by the recent labours upon it of an English artist,[1] which evidently portrays the Maha Hansa Jatak from the Jatakas or Birth-Tales.[2] These were the Puranas of Buddhism. That is to say, they were its popular literature. History is to a great extent merely the story of organisation, the gradual selecting and ordering of elements already present. And in that sense the Puranas form a reflection and imitation of the Jatakas. The elements of both were present before. Buddhism organised the one in Pali, and Hinduism, later, the other in Sanskrit. But in some cases it would appear as if the Mahavamsa, with its history of the evangelising of Ceylon, had been the treasure-house of Ajanta artists. There are in some of the caves, notably One, pictures of ships and elephant-hunts which seem to corre-

[1] See the reproduction in the *Burlington Magazine* for June 1910, together with Mrs. Herringham's valuable notes.

[2] Queen Khema has a dream about golden geese, and entreats Samyama the king to find one for her. The king has a decoy lake constructed and his fowler captures the king of the geese. The monarch is deserted by all his subjects save one, Sumukha, his chief captain. Then the two are brought before the king, who treats them with great honour, and when the goose-king has preached the law to him, they both return, with his permission, to their own kith and kin on the slopes of Chittrakuta.

"The Master here ended his story, and identified the Birth: at that time the fowler was Channa, Queen Khema was the nun Khema, the king was Sariputta, the king's retinue the followers of Buddha, Samukha was Ananda, and the Goose-king was myself. Maha Hamsa Jataka, p. 534. Vol. v. Cowell's Jataka.

spond to known fragments of that story. Yet again, in the same cave, there will be another picture of something frankly Puranic or Jatakyan,—such as the king stepping into the balances, in the presence of a hawk and a dove—and it is impossible in the present state of the paintings to make out the sequence. Here also occurs that political picture which dates the paintings of Cave One as after, but near, A.D. 626. It would be natural enough that the story of Ceylon should dispute with the Jatakas the interest of the Buddhist world. It formed the great romance of the faith. The same efforts had been made and as great work done in many other cases, but here was a country so small that the effort told. The whole civilisation yielded with enthusiasm to the stream of impulse that came to it from the home-land of its sovereigns. The Sacred Tree, with the prince Mahindo and the princess Sanghamitta, had formed an embassy of state of which any country might be proud. And the connection thus made had been maintained. We may imagine, if we please, that there were students from Ceylon here in the Sangharama of Ajanta. Kings and nobles would doubtless send their sons to the monasteries for education, even as is still done in the villages of Burma and Japan. The East was early literary in her standards of culture, and the fact that monastic instruction would no way have benefited a Norman baron need not make us suppose that the ministers and sovereigns of India, early in the Christian era,

MOTHER AND CHILD.

From Drawing by Nanda Lal Bose of the Fresco painting at Ajanta.

boasted an equally haughty illiteracy. The whole aspect of the caves, with the viharas containing the shrine of the Great Guru, tells us of the development which their functions had undergone, from being simple *bhikshugrihas* to organised colleges, under the single rulership of the abbot of Ajanta. Hiouen Tsang was only one out of a stream of foreign guests who came to the abbey to give knowledge or to gather it. And we must, if we would see truly, people its dark aisles and gloomy shadows with voices and forms of many nationalities from widely distant parts of the earth. In Cave One is an historical painting of the Persian Embassy which was sent by Khusru II to Pulakesin I about A.D. 626.

The cave I myself like least is Number Two. Here we have side-chapels containing statues of kings and queens or it may be pious patrons of less exalted rank, in one case with a child. The painting also in this cave has in some cases deteriorated in quality, although some great masterpieces are to be found here. There are parts where we can only think that a master has painted the principal figure and left the background or the retinue to be done by pupils or subordinates; and in some places we find foreshadowings of faults that were afterwards amongst the peasant painters to be carried far. There is an air of worldliness in placing the great of the earth almost in a line with the Master himself, though this must have been done long before the paintings were put on the walls, and the fact that some of these are also wanting in severity and style is a mere accident. There is another cave at the other end of the line where we find the same order of paintings as here. I think it must be Twenty-one. Indeed throughout the series from Nineteen to Twenty-six, any painting that remains is very inferior to that in Caves One to Seventeen. The subjects are full of life and energy. The fault is only that there is not the same learnedness and grandeur of treatment as in the best works of the Ajanta masters. Nowhere in the world could more beautiful painting be found than in the king listening to the golden goose in Cave Seventeen, or than the Masque of Spring—which I should have liked to interpret as the entrance of Queen Maya into the Garden of Lumbini—on the top of a pilaster in the same cave. According to the distinguished critic who has just been at work upon them, these pictures have many of the characteristics that appear almost a thousand years later in the best works of the great Italian masters. This is seen not only in general effects, but also in many of the details in method. The painters knew, for instance, how to graduate the outline so as to vary the intensity of its expression. And the same authority says that the anatomical knowledge shown in the modelling of limb and flesh is almost unapproachable. All this implies not only the advanced contemporary development of painting, but also the highest degree of concentration and respect for the work on the part of the worker.

It is this quality which seems somewhat to have lost its intensity in certain instances in Cave Two.

My own favourite amongst the caves is Four. But it is unfinished, and appears never to have been painted inside. Its proportions are wonderful—wide, lofty, vast. "This might have been our Westminster Abbey!" sighed an Indian fellow-guest, as we entered it for the first time. And the words exactly express it. It might have been India's Westminster Abbey.

But as they stand, it is Cave One that contains the masterpiece. Here on the left of the central shrine is a great picture, of which the lines and tints are grown now dim but remain still delicate. A man—young, and of heroic size—stands gazing, a lotus in his hand, at the world before him. He is looking down and out into the vihara. About him and on the road behind him stand figures of ordinary size. And in the air are mythical beings, *kinnaras* and others, crowding to watch. This fact marks the central personage as Buddha. But the ornaments that he wears as well as his tall crown show that we have here Buddha the prince, not Buddha the ascetic. A wondrous compassion pervades his face and bearing, and on his left—that is, to the spectator's right—stands a woman, curving slightly the opposite way, but seeming in every line to echo gently the feeling that he more commonly expresses. This picture is perhaps the greatest imaginative presentment of Buddha that the world ever saw. Such a conception could hardly occur twice. Nor is it easy to doubt, with the gate behind him and the waving palms of a royal garden all about him, that it is Buddha in that hour when the thought of the great abandonment first comes to him, Buddha on the threshold of renunciation, suddenly realising and pondering on the terrible futility of the life of man. His wife awaits him, gently, lovingly, yet with a sympathy, an heroic potentiality that is still deeper than all her longing sweetness. Yasodhara had a place, it seems, in the dreams of the monk-painters of Ajanta, and it was the place of one who could cling in the hour of tenderness, and as easily stand alone and inspire the farewell of a higher call. It was the place of one who was true and faithful to the greatness of her husband, not merely to his daily needs. It was the place of one who attained as a wife, because she was already great as a woman. These were the forms that looked down upon the noble Mahratta and Rajput[1] youth of the kingdom of the Chalukyas in their proudest days. Students trained here may have been amongst those who officered the constant wars of their sovereigns against the Pallavas of Conjeeveram, and repelled the invasions that began to fall upon India by the west coast from the late seventh century onwards. In their country homes in the rich Indian land, or round the bivouac fires on the field of battle in

[1] The Mahrattas are described as the people of the Ajanta country by Hiouen Tsang. The throne was held in the sixth, seventh, and eighth centuries by Chalukya Rajputs.

BUDDHA ON THE THRESHOLD OF RENUNCIATION.

From Drawing by Nanda Lal Bose of the Fresco painting at Ajanta.

the after-years, they would turn in their thoughts to these faces, speaking of a nobility and pity that stand alone in human history. A man is what his dreams make him. Can we wonder that that age was great in India whose dreams were even such as these?

THE CHINESE PILGRIM

AMONGST Indian historical documents there is none more fascinating than the books of their travels written by the early Chinese pilgrims. Of these the two now best known to us are those of Fa-Hian, who came to India about A.D. 400, and Hiouen Tsang, about A.D. 640. Hiouen Tsang, owing partly to the accident that his life was afterwards written by his disciples, appears to us as a personality, as the head and master of a large religious following, as a saint as well as a scholar, a monk as well as a traveller. But Fa-Hian is a lonelier, more impersonal figure. Monk and pilgrim as he was, it is rather the geographer that impresses us in him. Grave and sparing of words, he tells us little or nothing of himself. For all we know, he may have been the very first of the travellers who came to India on the task of Buddhistic research. From the surprise with which he is everywhere received and the complimentary exclamations that he records, it would appear indeed as if this had been so. On the other hand, from the quietness with which he comes and goes, from his silence about royal favours, and his own freedom from self-consciousness, it would seem as if the sight of Chinese visitors had not been rare in the India of that period, though the errand on which he and his party had come might single them out for some special degree of reverence and interrogation. "How great must be the devotion of these priests," said the people in the Punjab, "that they should have come thus to learn the law from the very extremity of the earth!" And yet frequent references to "the Clergy of Reason" in Kosala and in the south, these Clergy of Reason having apparently been Taoist monks on pilgrimage, involve a curious contradiction in this matter. Hiouen Tsang's is really a work of autobiography, but Fa-Hian's is rather the abstract of a statement made before some learned society, perhaps a university in the south of China, and countersigned by them.

In a certain year, with certain companions, Fa-Hian set out to make search in India for the Laws and Precepts of Religion, "because he had been distressed in Chhang'an (Sian in Shen-si, evidently his native province) to observe the Precepts and the theological works on the point of being lost, and already disfigured by lacunæ." Such are the quiet words with which the narrative begins. So colourless can be the phrases in which the passion of a life is stated. From that moment when Fa-Hian set out, to that other day when "at the end of the summer rest, they went out to meet Fa-Hian the traveller," who had surmounted obstacles incredible, and borne difficulties innumerable, was to be fifteen long years!

His book consists of some forty short chapters or paragraphs, each one dealing as a rule with a separate province or country. Of it he himself says:—

"The present is a mere summary. Not having been heard by the Masters hitherto, he (Fa-Hian) casts not his eyes retrospectively on details. He crossed the sea and hath returned, after having overcome every manner of fatigue, and has enjoyed the happiness of receiving many high and noble favours. He has been in dangers, and has escaped them. And now therefore he puts upon the bamboo what has happened to him, anxious to communicate to the wise what he hath seen and heard."

We can hardly doubt that this is a form of superscription, offering his paper on his travels to the consideration of some organised body of scholars.

Those travels themselves had occupied fifteen years. From the leaving of his native province of Chhang'an till his crossing of the Indus, "the river in the west," was a six years' journey. He spent six years in India itself, including two in Orissa. And finally, reckoning apparently two years spent in Ceylon, he was three years on the voyage home. Each stage of the journey is described, from the time of leaving Chhang'an. The kingdoms which he has traversed, he says in closing, number at least thirty. But, though the provinces south and west of Khotan are called "India of the North," he scarcely seems to think that he has reached India proper till he comes to Mathura. This he treats almost as if it were a capital. He seizes the moment of his arrival there to give one of his gem-like pictures of the whole country and its civilisation. He describes the Government, the freedom with which men come and go, untroubled by passport regulations, and the self-restraint with which justice is administered and the criminal punished. We must remember that these were the times of Vikramaditya, said to have been "of Ujjain." Was Ujjain, perhaps, the name of all Western India, and Mathura its metropolis? Compared with Mathura, Pataliputra appears relatively unimportant. It was older, grayer perhaps, and more imposing. It had been "the capital of Asoka." Its palaces were still marvellous. Ecclesiastically, too, it was strong as well as noted. Royal delegates were posted there from each of the provinces. But commercially, and perhaps even politically also, we feel that the centre of power in India was at the time of Fa-Hian's visit at Mathura. From this he makes his way, by Samkassa and Kanauj, into the heart of Buddha's own country—Sravasti, Kapilavastu, Kusinagara, and so on, down to Ganga, a chain of sites that by the painstaking labours of so many archæologists have now been in great measure recovered. From Ganga he returns to Pataliputra, and thence makes his way to Benares and Kausambi. Again making Pataliputra his headquarters, he seems to have spent three years in the Buddha country learning Sanskrit and copying manuscripts. And finally he sailed down the Ganges, through the kingdom of Champa, and came to Tamluk, or Tamralipti, where he stayed two years. When he left Tamralipti in a large ship for the south-west, he appears to have reckoned himself, though he was yet to spend two years in Ceylon, as already on the return journey.

The journey, as he describes it, constitutes an abstract of all that concerns Buddhism, and quietly ignores everything else in the country. "Brahmans and heretics" is Fa-Hian's comprehensive term for Hinduism in all its non-Buddhistic phases. We are able to gather a great deal nevertheless about the state of the country from his pages. In the first place we learn—as we do with still greater emphasis later from Hiouen Tsang—that to a learned Chinese, who had made an exhaustive study of Buddhism in Gandhara, and the kingdoms of the north-west frontier, India proper, or "India of the Middle," as he calls it, was still the country in which to seek for original and authentic images. Traversing Gandhara, Swat, Darada, Udyana, Takshasila, Purushapura, and Nagara (probably Kabul), it was not in any of these, but in Tamralipti that our traveller spent two years copying books and painting images. Again; already, at the time of Fa-Hian's visit, the old city of Rajgir, he tells us, is "entirely desert and uninhabited." It follows that the carvings and statuary in which to this day that site is rich are to a great extent of a school of sculpture which had grown, flourished, and decayed prior to A.D. 400. This in itself is a fact of immense importance. We constantly find in the travels that sacred places are marked by "*chapels*, monasteries, and stupas." Now a chapel of Buddha is undoubtedly an image-house. Nor is Fa-Hian himself entirely without feeling for the historical aspect of that Buddhistic sculpture which is one of the chosen objects of his study. He speaks always as if images were common enough in Buddhism, but he tells us that "the first of all images of Buddha, and that which men in aftertimes have copied," was a certain bull's head carved in sandal wood, which was made by Prasenajit, king of Kosala, at the time when Buddha was in the Tusita heaven preaching to his mother. The difference between an image and an emblem does not seem here to be very clearly apprehended, but the statement shows once for all that men in the fourth and fifth centuries looked to the eastern provinces, and to the country of Buddha's own activity, as the historic source of Buddhistic statuary. Again, when travelling in the kingdom of Tho-ly—north-east of the Indus, east of Afghanistan, and south of the Hindu Kush ; or, as has been suggested, Darada of the Dards—he tells us that there was once an *arhat* in this kingdom who sent a certain sculptor to the Tusita heaven to study the stature and features of Maitreya Bodhisattva. Three times the man went, and when he came down he made an image of heroic size, about eight English feet in height, which on festival days was wont to become luminous, and to which neighbouring kings rendered periodic worship. "This image," adds the pilgrim, in the far-away tone of one who speaks on hearsay, "still exists in the same locality." It was after the making of this statue, he further tells us, that the Buddhist missionaries began to come from the far side of the Indus, with their collections of the books and of the Sacred Precepts; and the image was erected three hundred years after the Mahanirvana. Here we learn a great deal. In the first place, when Buddhism crossed the Indus, three hundred years after the death of Buddha, it was already the religion of the Bodhisattvas. Obviously there had been solitary saints, and perhaps even communities of monastics, without the books before—or how should there have been an *arhat* to transport a sculptor three times to the Tusita Heaven?—but there was a sudden accession of Buddhistic culture at a date three hundred years after the death of the Master, and this culture was Mahayanist in character. Thus the Mahayana doctrine with its fully-equipped pantheon, its images, and its collections of books, to be declared canonical under Kanishka purported to come, like the Hinayana, from India proper, or, as Fa-Hian calls it, *Madhyadesa*. Magadha, Kosala, and Vaisali, then, may claim the honour of having initiated Buddhistic art as fully and truly as Buddhistic thought.

Further, it is clear that in Magadha itself the great ages of sculpture were felt to be already past. Talking of Pataliputra, which had been the capital of Asoka, "the palaces in the town have walls," says our traveller, "of which the stones were put together by genii. The sculptures and the carved work which adorn the windows are such as cannot be equalled in the present age. *They still exist.*" We who have seen the work done under Moghul emperors in marble, and the pierced sandstones of modern Benares, might not, had we seen them also, have been so ready as Fa-Hian to attribute a supernatural origin to the windows of the Asokan palaces. But the fact remains than an unimpeachable witness has assured us of the greatness and beauty of such work in Magadha, with the reputation of being ancient at the beginning of the fifth century A.D.

The great difficulty in the path of Fa-Hian was the scarcity of written documents. Everywhere he inquired for books, he tells us, but everywhere he found that the precepts were handed down by memory from master to disciple, each book having its given professor. At last, in the great temple of Victory in the Buddha country he found what he wanted, and there he stayed three years to copy. This is a most important light on many questions besides that with which it deals. It accounts, as nothing else could have done, for the tenacity with which the pure doctrine of Buddhism seems to have been held for so many centuries. The concentration of energy necessary for the carrying out of such a task as the memorising of a vast literature explains the gravity and decorum of the Orders so long maintained. "The decency, the gravity, the piety of the clergy," meaning the Buddhist monks, Fa-Hian takes several occasions to say, "are admirable. They cannot be described." It explains the tendency of Buddhistic monasteries to become universities. It explains the synthetic tendencies of the faith, which in the time of Kanishka could already include eighteen schools of doctrine declared to be mutually compatible, and not defiant. It also explains, turning to another subject altogether, why the first written version of the old Puranas should always so evidently be an edited version of an ancient original. It visualises for us the change from Pali to Sanskrit, and it justifies the sparseness of written archives in matters of Indian history. These were evidently memorised. On this point indeed Fa-Hian constantly tells us that kings granting lands to the Buddhistic orders engrave their deeds on iron, and we can only feel that as long as this was so, their non-survival is not to be wondered at. It must have been at a comparatively later period that brass and copper came to be used for a similar purpose, with the desired effect of permanence. Curiously enough, in Tamralipti there is no mention of difficulty regarding manuscripts. Nor again in Ceylon. In the last-named kingdom we know that the writing down had begun at least two or three centuries before the visit of Fa-Hian, and he would seem to have benefited by this fact. We gather then that as Magadha and Kosala were the source of Buddhistic doctrine in its different phases, and the source of successive waves of Buddhistic symbolism, so also they were the first region to feel the impulse of a literary instead of a verbal transmission of the canonical scriptures.

The difference between "India of the North"—or the Gandharan provinces beyond the Indus—and India proper in all matters of learning and the faith comes out very prominently in the pages of Fa-Hian, and ought to refute sufficiently all who imagine Gandhara as possessed of a culture in any way primary and impulsive, instead of entirely derivative and passive.

As if forecasting our need on this very point, the pilgrim particularly notes that on reaching India proper (and apparently in the great temple of Chhi'honan or Victory in Kosala) his last remaining companion, Tao-chhing, when he "beheld the law of the Shaneen, and all the clergy grave, decorous, and conducting themselves in a manner greatly to be admired, reflected, with a sigh, that the inhabitants of the frontiers of the kingdom of Thsin (China) were deficient in the Precepts and transgressed their duties; and said that if hereafter he could become Buddha, he wished that he might not be reborn in the country of the frontiers; on this account he remained, and returned not. Fa-Hian, whose first desire was that the precepts should be diffused and should penetrate into the land of Han, returned therefore alone."

About this same "India of the North" we have still more detail. The pre-Buddhistic Buddhism, which undoubtedly existed and was represented in Buddha's own day by his cousin Devadatta, was much more living in the Gandharan provinces at the time of Fa-Hian's journey than in India proper. Also the Birth Stories had become the romance of these provinces, and there were stupas there to the almsgiving of the eyes and of the head, to the giving of his own flesh by the Bodhisattva to redeem a dove, and to the making himself a meal for the starving tigress. We cannot help distinguishing between those countries whose Buddhism was Hinayana and those in which it was Mahayana, as more or less anciently the goal of Buddhist missions. And we note that Udyana, whose name seems to indicate that it had been a royal residence, perhaps the home-county, as it were, of the Kushan dynasty, was entirely Mahayana, and is mentioned under the name of Ujjana, as one of the northern *tirthas* in the Mahabharata. It would appear, indeed, that when the Himavant began to be parcelled out into a series of Mahabharata stations sometime under the later Guptas, the undertaking was in direct and conscious succession to an earlier appropriation of the regions further west, as stations of the Jatakas, or Birth stories of Buddha. We ought not, in the attempt to follow up some of the thousand and one threads of interest that our traveller leaves for us, to forget the one or two glimpses of himself that he vouchsafes us. Never can one who has read it forget the story of his visit to the cave that he knew on the hill of Gridhrakuta, where Buddha used to meditate, in Old Rajgir :

"Fa-Hian, having purchased in the new town perfumes, flowers, and oil lamps, hired two aged *bhikshus* to conduct him to the grots and to the hill Khi-che. Having made an oblation of the perfumes and the flowers, the lamps increased the brilliance. Grief and emotion affected him even to tears. He said: 'Formerly in this very place was Buddha. Here he taught the Sheou-leng-yan.[1] Fa-Hian, unable to behold Buddha in life, has but witnessed the traces of his sojourn. Still, it is something to have recited the Sheou-leng-yan before the cave, and to have dwelt there one night.'"

But Fa-Hian, enthusiast as he was, and capable of extreme exertions in the cause of the Faith and China, was not this alone. There was also in that grave and modest nature a chord that vibrated to the thought of home. "He longed ardently," he says, when he had already reached the South of China, "to see Chhang'an again, but, that which he had at heart being a weighty matter, he halted in the South where the masters published the Sacred Books and the Precepts." Thus he excuses himself for a brief delay on the way back to his native province. But if he feels thus when he has already landed on Chinese shores, what must have been his longing while still in foreign lands? In Ceylon, seated before the blue jasper image of Buddha, perhaps at Anuradhapura, he pauses to tell us:—

"Many years had now elapsed since Fa-Hian left the land of Han. The people with whom he

[1] The things which are difficult to discriminate from one another.

mingled were men of foreign lands. The hills, the rivers, the plants, the trees, everything that had met his eyes was strange to him. And what was more, those who had begun the journey with him were now separated from him. Some had remained behind, and some had died. Ever reflecting on the past, his heart was thoughtful and dejected. Suddenly, while at the side of this jasper figure, he beheld a merchant presenting in homage to it a fan of white lute-string of the country of Tsin. Without anyone's perceiving it, this excited so great an emotion that the tears flowed and filled his eyes."

Nor can we forget the simple and beautiful counter-signature which seems to have been affixed by the learned body to whom he presented it, to Fa-Hian's written summary of his travels. After telling how they met Fa-Hian and discoursed with him, interrogating him, and after telling how his words inspired trust, his good faith lent confidence to his recital, the scribe of the Chinese University, or Secretary to the Imperial Geographical Society, as it may have been ("the masters" in any case he calls them), ends thus :—

"They were touched with these words. They were touched to behold such a man : they observed amongst themselves that a very few had indeed expatriated themselves for the sake of the Doctrine, but no one had ever forgotten Self in quest of the law, as Fa-Hian had done. One must know the conviction which truth produces, otherwise one cannot partake of the zeal which produces earnestness. Without merit and without activity, nothing is achieved. On accomplishing aught, with merit and with activity, how shall one be abandoned to oblivion? To lose what is esteemed—to esteem what mankind forgot—Oh!"

THE RELATION BETWEEN BUDDHISM AND HINDUISM

BUDDHISM in India never consisted of a church but only of a religious order. Doctrinally it meant the scattering of that wisdom which had hitherto been peculiar to Brahman and Kshatriya amongst the democracy. Nationally it meant the first social unification of the Indian people. Historically it brought about the birth of Hinduism. In all these respects Buddhism created a heritage which is living to the present day. Amongst the forces which have gone to the making of India, none has been so potent as that great wave of redeeming love for the common people which broke and spread on the shores of Humanity in the personality of Buddha. By preaching the common spiritual right of all men whatever their birth, He created a nationality in India which leapt into spontaneous and overwhelming expression so soon as his message touched the heart of Asoka, the People's King. This fact constitutes a supreme instance of the way in which the mightiest political forces in history are brought into being by those who stand outside politics. The great Chandra Gupta, founding an Empire 300 B.C., could not make a nationality in India. He could only establish that political unity and centralisation in whose soil an Indian nationality might grow and come to recognise itself. Little did he dream that the germ of that Indian solidarity which was to establish his throne on adamantine foundations lay, not with himself, but with those yellow-clad beggars who came and went about his dominions, and threaded their way through the gates and streets of Pataliputra itself. Yet time and the hour were with him. He builded better than he knew. From the day of the accession of this Chandra Gupta, India was potentially mature. With the conversion of Asoka she becomes aware of her own maturity. Nothing appears more clearly in the mind of the great Asoka than his consciousness of the geographical extent and unity of his territory, and his sense of the human and democratic value of the populated centres. We find these things in the truly imperial distribution of his decrees; in the deep social value of his public works—roads, wells, hospitals, and the rest; and, above all, in the fact that he published decrees at all. Here was no throne-proud autocrat, governing by means of secret orders, but a sovereign, publishing to his people his notion of that highest law which bound him and them alike. Never did monarch live who so called his subjects into his councils. Never was there a father who more deeply gave his confidence to his children. Yet without the work done by Chandra Gupta the grandfather and completed by Asoka himself in his earlier years, in the long-repented conquest of Kalinga, or Orissa, this blossoming time of true nationality, when all races and classes of Indian folk were drawn together by one loving and beloved sovereign, would not have been possible. Asoka owed as much to the political unity of India as to the wondrous vision which he had received from Buddha of all that it means to be a man, a human being, high born or low born, Aryan or non-Aryan.

But the question, Of what spiritual confraternity did Asoka hold himself a member ?—becomes here of considerable importance. To belong to a new sect does not often have the effect of opening a man's heart to all about him in this fashion. Sects as a rule unite us to the few but separate us from the many. And here lies the meaning of the fact that Buddhism in India was no sect. It was a worship of a great personality. It was a monastic order. But it was not a sect. Asoka felt himself to be a monk, and the child of the monkhood, though seated on a throne, with his People as his church.

Similarly to this day there may at any time rise within Hinduism a great Sannyasin, whose fully-enrolled disciples are monks and nuns, while yet he is honoured and recognised as the teacher or *guru* by numberless householders. The position of the memory of Buddha as a Hindu teacher, in the third century before Christ, was not in these respects different from that of Sri Ramakrishna to-day, or that of Ramdas of Maharashtra in the seventeenth century. In the two last-named cases, however, the citizen-disciples, *Grihastha-bhaktas*, have a well-defined background in which they inhere. Hinduism is long ago a virtual unity—though that fact may not yet have been realised and defined—with its choice of religious systems to meet the needs of various types of character, and the great monastic *guru* stands outside all as a quickening and spiritualising force, whose influence is felt in each alike. The citizen-*bhakta* of Ramdas or Ramakrishna remains a Hindu.

In the days of Asoka, however, Hinduism was not yet a single united whole. The thing we now know by that name was then probably referred to as the religion of the Brahmans. Its theology was of the Upanishads. Its superstitions had been transmitted from the Vedic period. And there was as yet no idea that it should be made an inclusive faith. It co-existed with beliefs about snakes and springs and earth-worship, in a loose federation which was undoubtedly true to certain original differences of race.

With the age of Buddhism all this was changed. The time had now come when men could no longer accept their beliefs on authority. Religion must for all equally be a matter of the personal experience, and there is no reason to doubt the claim made by the Jainas, that Buddha was the disciple of the same *guru* as Mahavira. We know the age of a heresy by the tenets it contradicts, and in repudiating the authority of the Vedas,

Jainism proves itself the oldest form of nonconformity in India. And in the same way, by its relative return upon Vedic thought, we may find in Buddhism an element of reaction against Jainism. Only by accepting the Jaina tradition, moreover, as to the influence which their *gurus* had upon Buddha, are we able to account satisfactorily for the road taken by him from Kapilavastu to Bodh-Gaya through Rajgir. He made his way first of all to the region of the famous Jaina teachers. If, again, there should be any shred of truth in Sir Edwin Arnold's story (presumably from the Lalita-Vistara) that it was at Rajgir that He interceded for the goats, the incident would seem under the circumstances the more natural. He passed through the city on his way to some solitude where He could find realisation, with his heart full of that pity for animals and that shrinking from the thought of sacrifice, which was the characteristic thought of the age, one of the great preoccupations, it may be, of the Jaina circles He had just left. And with his heart thus full, He met the sacrificial herd, marched with them to the portals of Bimbisara's palace, and pleaded with the king for their lives, offering his own in their place. Whether this was actually so or not, it is certain that one of the great impulses of the day lay in the rebellion against the necessity of the Vedic sacrifice, one of its finest sincerities in that exaltation of the personal experience which made it seem natural to found on it a religion.

That a man's religious convictions must be the result of his own private realisation of truth is an idea so old in India as to lie behind the Upanishads themselves. But that such a realisation had a right to be socialised, to be made the basis of a religious sect, is a principle which was first perhaps grasped by the Jainas. It is this decision, thus definitely arrived at and clearly held, that accounts for the strength and certainty of Indian thought to this hour. For the doctrine that direct perception is the only certain mode of proof, and that all belief therefore rests on the direct perception of competent persons, is here unshakable; and it is easy to understand how such an attitude, on the part of a whole nation, exalts the individual thinker and the mind of genius.

The world is now so familiar with the spectacle of the religious leader going out from amongst his fellows and followed by all who think with him, to found some sect which is to be even as a new city of the human spirit, that it can hardly think itself back to the time when this was a thing unknown. In the age of the Vedas and Upanishads, however, the spectacle had not yet been seen in India. The religious teacher of those days lived retired in the forest clearings and gathered round him, not a sect, but a school, in the form of a few disciples. Jainism, with its sudden intense revolt against the sacrificial idea, and its sudden determination to make its pity effective for the protection of dumb animals, was the first religious doctrine to call social forces to its aid in India; in other words, it was the first organised sect or church, and by forming itself it invented the idea of sects, and the non-Jainas began to hold themselves in some sort of unity round the Aryan priesthood. Buddha in his turn accepted from Jainism its fearless pity, but not contented with the protection of the dumb creature, added to the number of those to be redeemed man himself, wandering in ignorance from birth to birth, and sacrificing himself at every step to his own transient desires. He realised to the full the career of the religious teacher as Jainism had made it possible, yet the doctrine which he preached as the result of his personal experience was in all essential respects identical with that which had already been elaborated in the forest-*ashramas* of the Upanishads, as the "religion of the Brahmans." It was in fact the spiritual culture of that period brought into being and slowly ripened in those *ashramas* of peaceful thought and lofty contemplation that pressed forward now to make the strength behind Buddha as a preacher. He declared that which the people already dimly knew. Thus, by the debt which he owes to both, this Great Sannyasin, calling all men to enter on the highest path, forms the bridge between the religion of the Aryans, tracing itself back to the Vedas, and the religion of the Jainas, holding itself to be defiant of the Vedas.

Such was the relation of Buddha to his immediate past, which he himself, however, overtopped and hid by his gigantic personality. We have next to look at the changes made by him in the religious ideas of succeeding generations. Taking Buddha as the founder, not of a sect, but of a monastic order, it is easy to see that his social organisation could never be cumulative. There must in fact come a time when it would die out. No new members could be born into his fold. His sons were those only on whom his idea had shone, those who had personally and voluntarily accepted his thought. Yet he must have had many lovers and admirers who could not become monastics. What was the place of the citizen-*bhaktas*, the *grihastha*-devotees of Buddha? We obtain glimpses of many such in the course of his own life. They loved him. They could not fail to be influenced and indeed dominated by him, in all their living and thinking thereafter. Yet they could not go out into the life of the wanderer, leaving the duties of their station. He was their sovereign, as it were, monarch of their souls. But he was not their general, for they were not members of the army. That place belonged only to monks and nuns, and these were neither.

Whatever was the place of the citizen-*bhakta*, it is clear that he would express in that place the full influence of the personal idea that Buddha represented. Not Indra of the Thousand Eyes, delighting in sacrifice, could ever again be the dream of the soul that had once loved Gautama. Calmness of meditation, light and stillness, detachment and knowledge, are now seen to be the highest powers of man. And this new realisation constantly reinforced by new admirers, will do its great work, not within the Buddhist order, but outside it, in the eventual modification of some other system. The conscious aim of the order as such will be to maintain its first condition of purity, truth, and ardour. The unconscious aim of the world without will be to assimilate more and more of the overflow of idealism that comes from within it, more and more of the personal impress left by One in whom all men's aspirations have been fulfilled. From this point we can see that the Order itself must some day die out in India, from sheer philosophical inanition and the want of a new Buddha. But its influence on the faiths outside it will echo and re-echo, ever deepening and intensifying.

Those faiths were, as we have seen, three in number—(1) Jaina; (2) Arya-Vedic; and (3) popular unorganised beliefs. It would appear, therefore, that the citizen-*bhakta* would necessarily belong to one or other of the groups. Already Jainism must have been a force acting, as we have seen, to unify the Arya-Vedic and the popular unorganised beliefs, giving its first impetus, in fact, to the evolution of what would afterwards be Hinduism, and this process Buddhism, with its immense aggressiveness for the redemption of man, would greatly intensify.

Yet the period would be considerable before this influence of the Buddhist idea would be sufficient to make itself perceptible in Hinduism, and its emergence, when that period was completed, might be expected to be abrupt.

My own opinion is that this influence makes itself visible in the sudden advent of the idea of Shiva or Mahadeva to a dominant position in the national life. In tracing out the evolution of the Shiva-image, we are compelled, I think, to assume its origin in the stupa. And similarly, in the gradual concretising of the Vedic Rudra into the modern Mahadeva, the impress made by Buddha on the national imagination is extraordinarily evident. Stirless meditation, unshadowed knowledge, fathomless pity, are now the highest that man can imagine of the soul. And why? For no reason, save that Buddha had gone to and fro for forty years after the attainment of Nirvana, and the print of his feet could by no means die out in India! The caves of Elephanta in the Bay of Bombay are a cathedral of Shiva-worship. They contain, moreover, not only an emblem of Shiva which may be more or less modern, but also a great many carvings. And none of these has a greater interest and importance than that on the left side of the entrance, a bas-relief of Shiva, wearing beads and tiger-skin, and seated in meditation. It is Shiva: it is not Buddha. But it is the Shiva of the Transition, and as such it is most significant.

For hundreds of years, then, before this emergence of Shiva as the main Hindu conception of God (which for a time he was), devout souls had loved Buddha and hastened with a special devotion to give alms to *sadhus,* without on that account suspecting for a moment that they were of any but the accepted Arya-Vedic household of faith. Less dependence on the great powers that dwelt beneath the mountain springs; less sense of the mystery of serpent and forest; an ever-deepening reverence for the free soul for the *sadhu,* for the idea of renunciation, this was all of which anyone was conscious. And yet in this subtle change of centres, history was being made; a new period was coming to the birth. Verily, those were great days in India between 500 B.C. and A.D. 200 or thereabouts. For the national genius had things all its own way, and in every home in the land the little was daily growing less, and the real and the universal were coming more and more prominently into view. Those were probably the days of *Gitas* made in imitation of the Buddhist *Suttas.* And this fact alone, if it be true, will give us some hint as to the preoccupation of the period with great thought.

"Thou that art knowledge itself,
Pure, free, ever the witness,
Beyond all thought and beyond all qualities,
To thee the only true Guru
My Salutation:
Shiva Guru! Shiva Guru! Shiva Guru!"

These words may be taken as the keynote of this first period in the making of Hinduism. The national faith will form itself henceforth like a great white SANKHA (conch-shell) coiled in broadening spirals about the Vedic pillar. The theological Iswara believed in by the Brahmans is referred to vaguely but conveniently by themselves and others at this time as Brahma. He is the God to whom the sacrifices are made. But in the presence of Buddha and the memory of Buddha a new and higher conception begins to prevail, and as time goes on this higher conception takes name and form as Shiva or Mahadeva. Hinduism is thus born, not as a system, but as a *process* of thought, capable of registering in its progressive development the character of each age through which it passes.

It follows, then, that the heirs of Buddha-*bhakti*, so to speak, in India, might be on the one hand Jainas, or on the other Saivite Hindus. These were the two churches whose children might be born as if in the shadow of Buddha. And it is in accordance with this that we find Saivism and Jainism subsequently dividing between them such places of Buddhist history as Benares and Rajgir.

ELEPHANTA—THE SYNTHESIS OF HINDUISM

At a great moment in the history of India the caves of Elephanta were carved out of the living rock. A moment of synthesis it was that ages had prepared; a moment of promise that would take milleniums to fulfil. The idea that we now call Hinduism had just arrived at theological maturity. The process of re-differentiation had not yet begun. The caves ot Elephanta mark perhaps its greatest historic moment. In all religious sects the conflict of opinion is determined more by the facts of history and geography than by opposing convictions. What then were the sources, geographic and historic, of the elements that make up Elephanta?

The caves themselves were meant to be a cathedral. So much is apparent on the face of things. Traces of palace, fortifications, and capital city must certainly be discoverable in their immediate neighbourhood. On another island several miles away is the Abbey of Kenheri with its chaitya hall and its 108 monastic cells, each two of which have their own water-supply; its bathing tanks, and refectory or chapter floors on the mountain-

Photo: Johnston and Hoffmann

CAVES OF ELEPHANTA

top. Kenheri was a university: Elephanta was a cathedral: and both were appanages of some royal seat.

How splendid is the approach through pillars to the great reredos in three panels that takes up the whole back wall of the vast cell! And in the porch, as we enter this central chamber, how impressive are the carvings to right and left! On the left, in low relief, is a picture representing Shiva seated in meditation. The posture is that of Buddha, and it requires a few minutes of close examination to make sure of the distinction. The leopard-skin, the serpents, and the *jata*, however, are clear enough. There is no real ground for confusion. On our right is another low relief of Durga, throwing herself into the universe, in God-intoxication. Behind her the very air is vocal with saints and angels chanting her praises. The whole is like a verse from *Chandi*. And we hold our breath in astonishment as we look and listen, for here is a freedom of treatment never surpassed in art, combined with a message like that of mediæval Catholicism. The artist here uttered himself as securely as the Greek. It was only in the thing said that he was so different. And for a translation of that into terms European, it needs that we should grope our way back to Giotto and Fra Angelico and the early painters of missals.

Our astonishment is with us still as we penetrate the shadows and find our way amongst the grey stone pillars to that point from which we can best see the great central Trimurti of the reredos. How softly, how tenderly, it gleams out of the obscurity! Shadows wrought on shadows, silver-grey against the scarcely deeper darkness; this in truth is the very Immanence of God in human life. On its right is the sculptured panel representing the universe according to the Saivite idea. Shiva and Parbati ride together on the bull, and again—as in the carving of Durga in the porch—the heavens behind them are like a chorus of song. On the left of the Trimurti, finally, is the portrayal of the world of the Vaishnavite. Vishnu the Preserver has for consort Lakshmi the Divine Grace and the whole universe seems to hail Him as God. It is the heads of Brahma, Shiva, and Vishnu, grouped together in one great image, that make up the Trimurti which fills the central recess between these panels.

A ledge for offerings runs along below this series of pictures. The altar itself, where actual consecration took place, is seen to the spectator's right, in the form of a little canopy-like shrine or Shiva chapel, which once doubtless held the four-headed Mahadev that may to-day be seen outside the caves, and now contains the ordinary image of Shiva, as placed there at some later date. We may assume that lights and offerings, dedicated here, were afterwards carried in procession, and finally placed before the various divisions of the great reredos. The pillared hall held the congregation, and stands for the same thing as the nave in a Christian church, or the courtyard in a modern temple like Dakkhineswar.

So much for the main cave. The plan of the entablature is carried out, however, in the architecture, and there are wings—consisting of cells built round courtyards enclosing tanks—to right and left of the great central chamber. And here the carved animals and other ornaments, that support short flights of stairs and terraces, are all eloquent of a great art period and a conception of life at once splendid and refined.

Elephanta, then, perpetuates the synthesis of Hinduism. How royal was the heart that could portray no part of his people's faith—even though it held his personal conviction and worship—without the whole! Not Saivite alone, but Saivite, Vaishnavite, and the still remembered worshipper of Brahma, go to make up the Aryan congregation. All alike, it is felt, must be represented. Nay, when we recall the older Kenheri, we feel that not the churches alone but also the monastic orders outside all churches; not society only but also the supersocial organisation, denying rank and all that distinguishes society, had a place here. In the architectural remains within a certain area of the Bay of Bombay, we have a perfect microcosm of the Indian thought and belief of a particular period. The question that presses for determination is, what was that period.

The first point to be noticed is the presence of Brahma in this synthesis of Hinduism. In the

Mahabharata, similarly, we are constantly startled by the mention of Brahma. He is there called the grandsire, the creator, and sometimes the ordainer, with face turned on every side. This last attribute is perhaps derived from some old mysticism, which gave the Romans Janus—from which our own January—and found expression amongst the Hindus in the four-headed image, and the weapon with four heads called Brahma's head, as mentioned in the Ramayana. While constantly referred to in the Mahabharata, however, Brahma is nowhere there invested with new functions. He does not appear as a growing concept of the divine. He plays rather the part of one receding from actuality who must constantly be held in memory. In the Puranic stories of Krishna, similarly, no one goes to Brahma with any prayer or austerity, as they do to Shiva. He is no dynamic factor in the life of men. Yet He *is* the Creator, beyond all argument. He is chief and eldest of Hindu post-vedic deities. His position needs no proving. It is accepted by all. Nor does Brahma in the Puranas require to be convinced that Vishnu is the equal of himself: Krishna, as the presentment of Vishnu, is new to him, but Vishnu himself He takes for granted. At the same time, while indisputably supreme, Brahma is by no means a spiritual reality. That place, as other stories and the whole of the Mahabharata show, is filled by Shiva, with whom are associated all those philosophical ideas nowadays described as Vedantic. And yet, if the story of

Krishna had been written in the twentieth century, Brahma would have had no place in it at all. Partially forgotten as He was then, He is wholly forgotten now. From this evidence then, we may infer that the personality of Brahma was the first, and that of Shiva the next, to be developed as concepts of Supreme Deity.

Thus there was a period in Hinduism when the name of Brahma the Creator was held in reverence —having dominated the theology of a preceding age—and used in conjunction with those of Shiva and Vishnu to make the specification of deity complete. Hinduism at that time deliberately preached God as the Three-in-One, the Unity-in-Trinity. This theological idea we find expressed in its purity in the Caves of Elephanta, and perhaps slightly later in the Ramayana of Valmiki.

The poet Kalidasa also, writing both the *Kumara-sambhava* and the *Raghuvamsa*, would appear to have been under the inspiration of this Hindu idea of the Trinity. He shared the desire of the power that carved Elephanta to represent the synthesis of Hinduism by doing something to concretise both its popular aspects.

But the form under which Vishnu appears in Elephanta is purely theological. It is Lakshmi-Narayana, the idea that to this day is more familiar to the West and South of India than to Bengal. This theological concept—or divine incarnation, as it is called—was fully formulated before the Ramayana was written, and is referred to there much oftener than in the Mahabharata; though that also was meant to prove the identity of a certain hero with Vishnu. Sita-Rama are from the very beginning argued as the bodying-forth of Lakshmi-Narayana in human form. Krishna in the later epic seems to be consciously a second attempt to paint the mercy of God in incarnation.

The ideas that succeed in India are always firm-based on the national past. Thus that idealism of the motherland which is to-day the growing force intellectually can go back for foundation to the story of Uma, wedded in austerity to the great God. Similarly it would be very interesting to see worked out by some Indian scholar the root-sources in Vedic literature of these conceptions of Shiva and Vishnu. One can hardly resist the conclusion that each was elaborated independently in its own region.

We have to think of the Mother Church as the expression of a people who, between 500 B.C. and A.D. 500, were intensely modern and alive. Indian civilisation has educated its children from the beginning to the supreme function of realising ideas. And ideas grew and succeeded each other, taking on new forms with amazing rapidity, in the period immediately before and after the Christian era. The impression that the chief formative impulse here was the life and character of Buddha is extremely difficult to resist. On one side the stern monastic; on the other, the very projection into humanity of the Infinite Compassion—the

Blessed One was both of these. His character was the world's proof that God was at once Preserver of His children, and Destroyer of their Ignorance, even while He was but a name for the Supreme itself. Hence in men's dreams of Shiva we see their effort thenceforth to realise the one, while Narayana is their personification of the other of these attributes.

Just as Buddha may have been the radiant centre whence diverged the popular religions, so Benares may have been the spot where the idea of Shiva was first conceived and elaborated. Many causes may have contributed to this. The Deer Park seven miles away must have been a monastic university before the time of Buddha. Its undisputed pre-eminence is shown by the fact that He made his way to it immediately on attaining enlightenment, because it was there that his theory, or discovery, must be published to the world. From this we can see that the monk, although a little apart, must always have been an impressive figure in Benares, which was itself, at this particular period, mainly a commercial and industrial centre, associated with a great Brahmanic wealth of Vedic memory.

After the time of Buddha, while his name still reverberated throughout the length and breadth of the land, Benares would doubtless become a place of pilgrimage, rendered doubly sacred by his memory and by its Vedic altar. The growing opinion that the Deity could take no delight in slaughter must have killed the sacrifices, and the Brahmans of Benares would take to cherishing a system of theology in which the great God was represented as remote, solitary, and meditative. The right of all classes to interest themselves in religious philosophy was indisputable, in face of the work done by the Buddhist Orders, and Vedantic theories and explanations were given freely to all comers, and by them carried back over the country to their distant homes.

We may suppose, meanwhile, that the memorial stupas continued to be placed in the sacred city, as at other scenes of Buddhist memory, by pious pilgrims. Little by little the stupas changed their shape. At first plain, or simply ornamented, they came to have the four Buddhas on them, looking North, South, East and West. Some were then made, by a natural transition, with four large heads instead of four seated figures. According to the Brahmans, the God of the Aryans was Brahma, the personal aspect of Brahman. According to the thought of the world at that period, again, God, or Brahma, was "the Ordainer, with face turned on every side." Hence the four-headed stupa was first, perhaps, regarded as the image of Brahma. But it could not long be so taken. The new conception of God was growing, and presently, with the post in the middle, it came to be regarded as Mahadeva, and then as Shiva.

There was a good deal of hesitation at this period. Anyone who has seen the bathing *ghât* at Baragaon, between Behar and Rajgir, will be in a position to judge in how many different directions the emblem of Shiva might have been evolved. The four-headed stupa, for instance, was sometimes made to refer to Parvati. Finally, however—with the perfecting of the theological idea of Maheswara—the modified stupa was taken as Shiva. This particular phase must have occurred just as the Rajputs began to settle in Rajputana, and this accounts for the prevalence of the four-headed Shiva in that country. The family-God of the royal line of Udaipur is said to be a four-headed Mahadeva. In Benares again there may be more, but there is certainly one temple in the Tamil quarter behind the monastery of Kedar Nath, where a Shiva of the period in question is worshipped to this day. When first erected this temple was doubtless on a level with the street. Owing to the accumulation of debris in the interim, however, it is now some eight or ten steps down. This fact alone gives us some notion of the age of the building.

The image of Mahadeva has gone through many further phases of simplification since the day we speak of, but this Shiva of Benares and the other of Elephanta belong to a single historic period, and the small four-headed stupa outside the caves is one of their most precious relics.

Hinduism throbs with the geography and history of India. In every image of Shiva speaks the voice of pre-Gupta Benares. In that complex conception of Krishna which blends in one the Holy Child of Brindaban, the Hero of the *Gita*, and the Builder of Dwarka, we celebrate the vision of the royal house of Pataliputra. In the Ramayana we unravel the earlier dream of Kosala. And here in Elephanta on the extreme West, we are confronted with a rendering of the great synthesis that comes after the formulation of Shiva. Whence did Elephanta take her Lakshmi-Narayana? And what must have been the solidarity of the country when the dream dreamed in Benares finds expression here a thousand miles away!

Wherever we turn we are met by the same phenomenon of the marvellous and effective unity of pre-mediæval India. The Narayana, who is constantly worshipped in Madras, is the same whose images were wrought in Behar so long ago as the fifth century. A single style of architecture characterises a single period, from Bhubaneshwar to Chitore. Every child knows the names of the seven sacred rivers; and the perfect *tirtha*, for every province of India, has taken a man these many centuries to the Himalayas, to Dwarka, to Cape Comorin, and to Puri.

SOME PROBLEMS OF INDIAN RESEARCH

ONE of the first tasks before the Indian people is the rewriting of their own history. And this, in accordance with the tacit rule of modern learning, will have to be carried out, not by one, but by a combination of individuals; in other words, by an Indian learned society. It is a strange but incontrovertible truth, that none of us knows himself unless he also know whence he arose. To recognise the geographical unity and extent of the great whole we call India is not enough; it is imperative also to understand how it came to be.

Fortunately we are now in possession of a single precious volume—*The Early History of India*, by Vincent Smith—of which it may roughly be said that it embodies the main results of the work concerning India done during the last century by the Royal Asiatic Society. We must be grateful for so handy a compendium summarising for and opening to the Indian worker the results achieved by the European organisation of research, as nothing else could have done, save that personal intercourse with great scholars which is at present beyond his reach. Vincent Smith's work may seem to some of us, considering its scope and subject, to be curiously unspiritual. Yet is it the veritable handing on to a new generation of scholars of the torch of the spirit.

Nothing surely in all the story here told of early India is more inspiring than that of the Guptas of Magadha and the empire which they, from their ancient seat of Pataliputra, established over the whole of India. The central fact about this great Gupta Empire, as it will seem to Indian readers, is the identification of Vikramaditya, who is now seen to have been "of Ujjain" merely in the familiar modern sense of the title added to the name of the conqueror. Vikramaditya of Ujjain, then, was no other than Chandragupta II of Pataliputra, who reigned from A.D. 375 to A.D. 413.

If this was so, we might take the year A.D. 400 as a sort of water-parting in the history of the development of modern India. The desire becomes irresistible to know how far the Puranic Age was then developed and established; to what extent and under what form Buddhism was still remembered; what was the political outlook of a Hindu of the period; and, among the most important of the questions to be answered, what were the great cities that made up the Indian idea of India, and what the associations of each? The answer to the last of these queries, if discoverable at all, would be of vastly greater significance than all the facts as to sovereigns and kingdoms about which the modern system of learning makes us so unduly curious.

It is already a commonplace among historians that Hinduism, together with Sanskrit learning and literature, underwent under the Guptas what is regarded as a great revival. According to Vincent Smith, most of the Puranas were during this period re-edited and brought into their present shape. Statements of this kind are at present somewhat vague, but accepting what has already been done as our basis, it will, I believe, prove possible to introduce a definiteness and precision into the history of the evolution of Hindu culture which has not hitherto been dreamed of as practicable. We shall soon be able to follow step by step, dating our progress as we go, the introduction of one idea after another into the Hindu system, building up again the world which surrounded the makers of the Puranic age.

In Vincent Smith's pages we can see the great tradition of Gupta learning beginning in the person of the gifted and accomplished Samudra Gupta (A.D. 326 to A.D. 375), father of Vikramaditya, and a sovereign of such military ability as to be described as "an Indian Napoleon," while he himself had the fine ambition to be remembered rather for his love of music and poetry than for his success in war. In the reign of such a king, and in the personal influence of such a father, must have lain the seed of more achievements and events which were to make his son Vikramaditya the hero of

Indian tradition through subsequent ages. It takes many lives sometimes to carry out a single great task, and we can only guess whether or not Samudra Gupta began the undertakings whose completion was to make his son illustrious.

In my own opinion, the very head and front of these must have been the final recension of the Mahabharata at some time within the famous reign, say at about the year A.D. 400. It is difficult to resist the conclusion that certain of the Puranas, notably the *Vishnu* and *Bhagavata*, were edited, exactly as the Bhagavata claims, immediately after the Mahabharata by scholars who found cause for regret in the fact that work had not given them the scope required for all the details they were eager to give regarding the life of the Lord. I do not remember even to have seen any note on the social functions of the Puranas. But the Vishnu Purana strongly suggests a state curriculum of education. In the ages before printing, literature must for the mass of people in all countries have tended to take the form of a single volume—witness the name *biblos* or Bible, *the* book—containing elements of history and geography, a certain amount of general information, some current fiction, and above all an authoritative rendering of theology and morals in combination. History of course would be reduced to little more than an indication of the origin of the reigning dynasty, or a sketch of the epoch regarded at the time of writing as "modern." Geography would consist of an account of the chief pilgrimages and sacred rivers. And in the Vishnu Purana, in the stories of Dhruva and Prahlada, when compared with the infinitely superior popular versions, we have a key to the treatment which fiction and folklore would receive. As the theological exposition proceeds, one can almost see the Brahman teaching at the temple-door while the shades of evening gather, and ignoring every other consideration in his desire to put the highest philosophy into the mouth of Prahlad, or to pin a religious meaning to the astronomical picture of the child Dhruva pointed onwards by the Seven Rishis.

It would be clearly impossible for every village in the Gupta Empire to possess either a scholar learned in, or a copy of, the Mahabharata. But the scheme of culture comprised in the knowledge of the work known as the Vishnu Purana was not equally unattainable; and it is difficult to resist the conclusion that the book was planned or edited as a standard of common culture. If there be anything in this suggestion, a new importance will be conceded to the question of the province or district in which each separate Purana was produced. A single touch in the Vishnu Purana is sufficient to indicate its composition in the neighbourhood of an imperial capital, such as Pataliputra must have been. This is found in the story of Hiranyakasipu taking his little son on his knee, when he had been under tuition for some time, and putting him through his catechism. One of the questions in this catechism is extremely suggestive. "How should one deal with an enemy by whom one is vastly outnumbered?" asks the father. "Divide and attack them one by one," answers the son, evidently from his book. In Hindu literature there is no second work which can be called "national" in the same sense as the Mahabharata. The foreign reader, taking it up as sympathetic reader merely and not as scholar, is at once struck by two features; in the first place, its unity in complexity; and in the second, its constant effort to impress on its hearers the idea of a single centralised India with an heroic tradition of her own as formative and uniting impulse. It is in good sooth a monarch's dream of an imperial race. The Gupta Emperor of Pataliputra who commissioned the last recension of the great work was as conscious as Asoka before him or Akbar after of making to his people the magic statement, "India is one."

As regards the unity of the work itself, this in the case of the Mahabharata is extraordinary. That a composition so ancient in subject-matter, and so evidently complex in its derivation, should be handed down to us as one single undisputed whole, is historical evidence of the highest importance for its original promulgation in this form by some central power with ability and prestige to give it authoritative publication. The origins of the poem are hoary with antiquity. Its sources are of an infinite variety. But the Mahabharata was certainly wrought to its present shape in the shadow of a throne, and that imperial. So much is clear on the face of it to one who meets with the book for the first time in mature life.

One would naturally expect it to have existed in fragments, or at best to be current in many different versions. Indeed it is clear enough on the reading, that it has at some far past time so existed. Every here and there the end of one chapter or canto will tell a tale in one way, and the beginning of the next repeat it, or some part of it, from an utterly different point of view, as might rival narrators of a single incident. But the work of collating and examining, of assigning their definite values to each separate story, and weaving all into a single co-ordinated whole, has been done by some one great mind, some mighty hand, that went over the ground long long ago, and made the path that we of to-day must follow still. The minute differences of reading between the Bombay and Benares texts only serve to emphasize this single and uncontested character of one immortal rendering of the great work. All through Maharashtra and the Punjab, and Bengal and *Dravida-desh*, the Mahabharata is the same. In every part of India and even amongst the Mohammedans in Bengal it plays one part—social, educational, man-making, and nation-building. No great man could be made in India without its influence upon his childhood. And the hero-making poem is one throughout every province of the land.

Socially the first point that strikes one, as one

reads, is the curious position held by the Brahman. It is very evident that this is as yet by no means fixed. No duty with which an audience was already familiar would be so harped upon as is that of gifts to and respect for the Brahmans here. We notice too that the caste is not yet even fixed, for Draupadi is represented at her *swayamvara* as following the five brothers, when she and everyone else imagine them to be Brahmans. Nor is this a detail which requires explanation or apology, as does the marriage of one woman to five men. No, at the date of the last recension of the Mahabharata, a marriage between Brahman and Kshatriya is well within the understanding and sympathy of an audience. It is however fairly clear that the promulgation of the work is bound up with the success of the Brahmans in impressing themselves and it on the public mind. It was entrusted to them, perhaps by royal warrant—even as in the story of Damayanti another story is given to them to carry forth of her father's capital—to spread far and wide, depending on the alms of the faithful for payment. And we are constrained at this point to ask, What up to this moment had been the characteristic work of the Brahmans as a caste?

But there are notable exceptions to this constant commendation of the Brahmans to the consideration and charity of their hearers. On looking closer, we find that there are many passages of no inconsiderable size in which the Brahmans are never mentioned. And this feature gradually establishes itself in our minds as a very good *differentia* of the more modern additions. It would appear that in its earlier versions the poem contained no forced mention of this particular caste, and that, in making the final recension, some care was observed to maintain the purity of the ancient texts, even while incorporating with them new matter and new comments.

The most important question of all however is one on which a new reader will find it hard to imagine himself mistaken. This is the question as to who is the hero of the last recension. Undoubtedly the Mahabharata, as we have it, is the story of Krishna. It is difficult to understand how the theory could have been put forward that the final editing had been Saivite. On the contrary, Mahadeva is represented as speaking the praises of Krishna, while, so far as I am aware, the reverse never happens. This could only mean that Hinduism as it stood was here, in the person of Shiva, incorporating a new element, which had to be ratified and accepted by all that was already holy and authoritative. The Krishna of the national story is indeed Partha-Sarathi the Charioteer of Arjuna—most probably an earlier hero of Dwarka and the war-ballads—but every effort is made, by calling him Keshava and the slayer of Putana, to identify him with that other Krishna, hero of the Jumna, who appears to have been worshipped by the cowherds, a people still half-nomadic as it would seem, who must have been established peacefully in India some centuries before his time.

Was Krishna Partha-Sarathi, then, the deliberate preaching of the Gupta dynasty to the (at that time half-Hinduised) peoples of the south side of the Jumna? Was he a hope held out to the democracy, a place made in the national faith for newly imperialised populations? Was it at this period that the play of the Mahabharata was deliberately established as an annual *Pandava-lila* in the villages of the south, while to Krishna Partha-Sarathi especially temples were built in *Dravida-desh?* In any case, there is abundant evidence half a century later, when we pass to the reign of Skanda Gupta the grandson of Vikramaditya, of the hold which the Krishna of the Jumna had obtained over the hearts of the imperial house of Pataliputra at Bhitari.[1] In the district of Ghazipur to the west of Benares is still standing a pillar which was raised by the young king on his return from victory over the Huns in A.D. 455. He hastened to his mother, says the inscription, "just as Krishna, when he had slain his enemies, betook himself to his mother Devaki." The pillar was erected to the memory of his father—it may have marked the completion of the requiem ceremonies postponed by war—and in commemoration of the victory just gained by the protection of the gods. It was surmounted finally by a statue of the god Vishnu. This statue has now disappeared, but we

[1] Vincent Smith. *Early History of India*, pp. 267–8.

may safely infer that it was of the form still common in the south of India as that of Narayana. It was probably made in low relief on a rounded panel, and depicted a beautiful youth with a lotus in his hand. In the following year 456 a great piece of engineering, so far west as the Girnar Hill, was completed and consecrated by the building of a temple of Vishnu.

Seven hundred and fifty years earlier, in the year 300 B.C., Megasthenes had noted amongst Indian religious ideas that "Herakles is worshipped at Mathura and Clisobothra." Was this latter the Hellenic pronunciation of "Klisoputa," Krisoputra, Krishnaputa? And is it to be identified with Dwarka, persistently identified with Krishna throughout the Mahabharata without any very satisfactory reason being stated—or with some other town near Mathura, since destroyed?

Now this same Herakles is a figure of wonderful interest. We must remember with regard to the period of which we are now thinking, that Greece was but the remotest province of the Central Asiatic world, and in that world the youngest child of history. Her myths and religious systems had chiefly a central Asiatic origin, and Herakles of Mediterranean fame was doubtless pre-eminently of this order. Probably little ever finds its way into literature of the human significance to human souls of any given religious system, or more particularly of the ideas connected with an ancient god or hero. We may depend upon it that Herakles of Hellas, when he was worshipped by the common folk, had more in him of the Christ who saves, more of the Krishna, lover of man, than any of us now could easily imagine.

It may be that Krishna slaying the tyrant of Mathura forms but another echo of some immeasurably ancient tale, held by future nations in common, ere the Asian tablelands or the Arctic home had poured down new-born breeds of man on the coasts of Greece and river-banks of India. So at least must it have seemed to Megasthenes, making up his despatches for Seleukos Nikator. And 700 years go by, it appears, before a Gupta emperor, who has just annexed Western India with its capital of Ujjain, commissioned the editing anew of the national epic of the north, causing it to teach that this Cliso—Kriso—Krishna of the Jumna is no other than a certain Partha-Sarathi, known this long while to Northern and Vedic India as the exponent to his disciples of all the secrets of the Upanishads. Are we to take it that the Aryan teacher cries, "Whom ye ignorantly worship, Him declare I unto you" to the tribes whom he fain would Hinduise?

Readers of the *Bhagavata Purana* will note that the Jumna life, that is to say, the Heraklian element in the story of Krishna, is crowded into his first twelve years and that after this he is represented as *being sent to learn the Vedas.* That is to say, it is at this point that he is Hinduised as the Incarnation of Vishnu. Obviously, after this had been done, many of the incidents of his childhood might have a Hindu interpretation reflected back upon them.

How great is the beauty of that divine childhood! How warm and throbbing the sense of personality that speaks in every line of the Mahabharata! In spite of the English dress, how wonderful the power and passion with which both Epic and Purana tell the tale of Krishna! How rude yet grand this ancient world out of which in its unsuspecting simplicity, in its worship of strength and heroism, comes the story of the Lord slaying demon upon demon, elephant, wrestler, tyrant, all. Centuries, maybe milleniums, will go by before the tender Hinduising interpretation will be added to each incident, "and then, offering salutation at the feet of Krishna, the soul of that evil one went forth unto bright places, for ever the touch of the Lord brought salvation, even unto those whom He appeared to slay."

Like children long ago on the Greek islands, and children and men in German Scandinavian forests, or like the peasants of to-day in Icelandic log-houses, so have the Indian people all down the centuries listened to wonder-tales of a hero who was vulnerable at no point save on the soles of his feet; of mortals who went armed with divine weapons; of that strong one who could gulp down the forest-fire like water; of the woman who peeped and saw between her eyelids; of madness sent by the gods upon whole peoples whom they would slay; of dooms and destinies and strange heroic whispers from the twilight of the world.

But nowhere, it seems to me, does the enthusiasm of the story carry us so completely away as when we read at last of the ascension of Krishna into heaven. Here we are dealing with nothing prehistoric. Here we have the genius of a great Hindu poet in full flight. All that the ecclesiasticism of the West has done in fifteen centuries to place the like incident in the Christian story in an exquisite mystical light, half-veiled by its own glory, was here anticipated by some unnamed writer of the Gupta era in India, in or before the year A.D. 400, ending the story of the Incarnation on a note of mingled love and triumph:

"And He the Lord, passing through the midst of Heaven, ascended up into His own inconceivable region. Then did all the immortals join together to sing His praises. The gods and the rishis likewise offered salutation. And Indra also, the king of Heaven, hymned Him right joyfully."

THE FINAL RECENSION OF THE MAHABHARATA

We may take it then, for the sake of the argument, that the final recension of the Mahabharata was the literary *magnum opus* of the reign of Chandra Gupta II of Magadha, known as Vikramaditya of Ujjain (A.D. 375 to 413), and the source of his great fame in letters. We may also take it from the evidences seen there that he deliberately organised its promulgation by missions in the *Dravida-desh*, or country of the *Madras*. But, if all this be true, what may we suppose to have been the means employed by him for the execution of so vast an undertaking? Undoubtedly the work of compilation must have been carried out in Benares by a council of scholars under the control of one supreme directing genius. If Professor Satis Chandra Vidyabhushan be correct (as I should imagine that he is) in his suggestion that the name of *Devanagari*, as applied to one particular form of Prakrit script, means of *Devanagar* or Benares,[1] the question then arises, Was the promulgation of the Mahabharata the occasion on which it gained its widespread fame and application?

[1] See *Indian World*, November, 1906.

The possible date of the Ramayana suggests itself at this point as a subject for examination and decision. For my own part, trying the question on grounds other than that of language, I would suggest that the first part of this work was written *before* the Mahabharata was finally edited, and that it opens up a long vista of years during which Ayodhya had already been the principal Indian capital. The hypothesis is thus that the Asokan capital of Pataliputra was succeeded by Ayodhya, and this again succeeded, under the Guptas by Pataliputra. I am assuming that the *Uttarakanda* portion of the Ramayana was written later, according to what is said to be the tradition of the islanders of Baly and Lombok, east of Java. The fact that a synopsis of the Ramayana as it then stood is given in the Mahabharata, even as Kalidas's *Kumara Sambhava* is epitomised in the Ra.nayana, points possibly to some literary convention of an age when books were necessarily few. One cannot help feeling that it is the political greatness of Ayodhya and Pataliputra, each in its own period, that leads it to preach a new religion in the form of a definite incarnation of Vishnu—in the one case Rama, in the other Krishna. And if this be true, it lends an added interest to the fact that the worship of Sita-Rama has now its greatest following in the *Dravida-desh*. We may take it perhaps as a law that a religion is likely to survive longest and with greatest power, not in the region of its birth, but in the land to which it is *sent* or *given.* An exception is found in the worship of Shiva, which is still dominant in Benares.

If the date I have suggested as that of the final compilation of the Mahabharata be correct, it would follow that the great work must in the doing have trained a vast number of scholars and critics. It must also have called together in one place (doubtless Benares) an enormous mass of tradition, folk-lore, old records, and persons representing various kinds of ancient knowledge. All this would constitute that city an informal university of a most real and living type, and it might well be that the learning and research of which to this day it is the home was the result of the revival thus created under Vikramaditya of Ujjain.

Of the Gupta age as a whole (A.D. 326 to 500), we find Vincent Smith saying:—

"To the same age probably should be assigned the principal Puranas in their present form; the metrical legal treatises, of which the so-called Code of Manu is the most familiar example; and, in short, the mass of the 'classical' Sanskrit literature. The patronage of the great Gupta emperors gave, as Professor Bhandarkar observes, 'a general literary impulse,' which extended to every department, and gradually raised Sanskrit to the position which it long retained as the sole literary language of Northern India. . . . The golden age of the Guptas, glorious in literary, as in political, history, comprised a period of a century and a quarter

(330 to 455 A.D.), and was covered by three reigns of exceptional length. The death of Kumâra, early in 455, marks the beginning of the decline and fall of the empire."[1]

And again :—

"The principal Puranas seem to have been edited in their present form during the Gupta period, when a great extension and revival of Sanskrit Brahmanical literature took place."[2]

The revision and re-editing of records thus described would be an inevitable result of the royal recension of the Mahabharata, supposing that to have taken place, nor is it necessary, in my own opinion, to mass the writings in question together as "the principal Purânas," for it is possible to trace a serial development of the Hindu idea, which makes it easy enough to distinguish chronological periods in Puranic literature, with a considerable approach to definiteness.

With regard to the Mahabharata itself, if the theory suggested as to the date of its last recension should be finally accepted, it will, I believe, prove not impossible so to determine its different strata as to be fairly sure what parts were added in the Gupta period, and by the Gupta poet. We must remember that Indian students might easily qualify themselves, as no alien could, to apply the tests of language and theological evolution. This and similar work might easily be undertaken by literary

[1] *Early History of India*, pp. 267–8.
[2] *Ibid.*, p. 19.

societies. And I would suggest—in accordance with a method already widespread in Biblical criticism—that students' editions of the texts might be printed, in which the ground of pages and paragraphs should be of various colours, according to their supposed periods. The paper of indeterminate passages might be white, for instance, the ancient yellow, the Saivite green or pink, and the additions of the Gupta period blue in tint. Or students might carry out this somewhat elaborate undertaking for themselves by means of washes of colour. In any case, such a device would prove a valuable mode of presenting to the eyes at a single glance the results of considerable time and labour.

Some points in the relative chronology are easy enough to determine. The story of Nala and Damayanti, for instance, by the exquisite prayer of Nala—"Thou blessed one, may the Adityas, and the Vasus, and the twin Ashwins, together with the Marutas, protect thee, thine own honour being thy best safeguard!"—betrays the fact of its origin in the Vedic or Upanishadic pre-Puranic period. The story of Nala and Damayanti is one of the oldest of Aryan memories, and the mention of the man's name first may be a token of this. The atmosphere of the story is that of the India in which Buddhism arose. The king cooks meat, and his wife eats it. The gods who accompany Nala to the *Swayamvara* are Vedic gods. There is no allusion throughout the story to Mahadeva or Krishna. There is, on the other hand, a serpent possessed of mysterious knowledge. And the Brahmans are represented as servants, not as governors, of kings. One of the next stories, in that wonderful *Vana Parva* in which Nala and Damayanti occurs, is the tale of Sita and Rama. And third and last of the series is Savitri. This sequence is undoubtedly true to the order of their evolution. Sita is the woman of sorrow, the Madonna of serenity. And Savitri, which is late Vedic, and referred to in the Ramayana—showing little or no trace of Saivite or Vaishnavite influence, save perhaps in the mention of Narada—is the fully Hinduised conception of the faithful wife. Her birth as the incarnation of the national prayer is an instance of the highest poetry. And the three heroines together—Damayanti, Sita, Savitri—constitute an idealisation of woman to which I doubt whether any other race can show a parallel.

That such tales as the *Kirat-Arjuniya*, again, belong to the Saivite recension, there can be no question. Equally certain is it, that some incidents, such as that of Draupadi's cry to Krishna for protection, and Bhishma's absorption in Krishna on his death-bed, must belong to the Gupta version. The rude vigour of the gambling scene, however, and the old warrior's death on the bed of arrows, as well as the marriage of five Pandavas to one queen, would appear to come straight out of the heroic age itself.

It would greatly aid us in our conception of

the genius and personality of that unknown poet who presided over the deliberations of the Council of Recension, if we could say with certainty what touches in the great work were his. Was he responsible, for instance, for that supremely beautiful incident, according to which, up to a certain moment, the wheels of Yudhisthira's chariot had never touched the earth? If so, the world has seen few who for vigour and chastity of imagination could approach him. But not alone for the purpose of literary appreciation would one like to divide the great poem into its component strata. We are familiar with the remark that while the things *stated by* works of the imagination are usually false, what they *mention* is very likely to be true. It is the things mentioned in the Mahabharata that demand most careful analysis. Of this kind are the various references to the cities of the period.

Although the centre of the events which the work chronicles is supposed to lie at Hastinapura or Indraprastha in the remote past, we are made constantly aware that the poet himself regards the kingdom of Magadha as the rival focus of power. Jarasandha may or may not have lived and reigned during the age of Krishna and the Pandavas. What is clear is that the last compilers of the Mahabharata could not imagine an India without the royal house of Rajgir. The same fact comes out with equal clearness in the *Bhagavata Purana* and possibly elsewhere. Now this is a glimpse into the *political* consciousness of the Gupta period. It shows us Northern India, then as now, dominated by two governing forces—one seated near Delhi, and one within the region to-day known as Bengal; and it shows unity to be a question mainly of a coalition between these two. Two hundred and fifty years later than Vikramaditya, India is again ruled by a strong hand, that of Harishchandra. But his capital is at Thaneswar, near Kurukshetra. Thus the shifting and re-shifting goes on, and the great problem of modern times, that of finding a common sentiment of nationality, is seen to be but a new inclusion of an age-old oscillation of centres, whose original cause may perhaps be deep-hidden in the geographical and ethnological conditions that gave birth to India.

Why, again, is the scene of the telling of the Mahabharata laid, theoretically, at Taxila? This place, situated to the north-west of Rawal Pindi, would appear, from the age of Buddha onwards till the coming of the Huns more than a thousand years later, to have occupied much the same place in Indian parlance as the University of Cordova in mediæval Europe, and for much the same reason. The city was a university in the time of Buddha, as witness the youth who went there from Rajgir to learn medicine. It lay on the highway of nations. Past its very doors streamed the nomadic hordes of invading Scythian and Tartar, both before and after the birth of the Christian era. Long before that it had given hostelry and submission to the Greek raid under Alexander. In mediæval Europe, similarly, medicine could be learnt at Cordova, because there was the meeting-place of East and West. In the Moorish university African, Arab, Jew, and European all met, some to give, others to take, in the great exchange of culture. It was possible there to take as it were a bird's-eye view of the most widely separated races of men, each with its characteristic outlook. In the same fashion, Taxila in her day was one of the focal points, one of the great resonators, as it were, of Asiatic culture. Here, between 600 B.C. and A.D. 500, met Babylonian, Syrian, Egyptian, Arab, Phœnician, Ephesian, Chinese, and Indian. The Indian knowledge that was to go out of India must first be carried to Taxila, thence to radiate in all directions. Such must have been the actual position of the city in the Hindu consciousness of the Gupta period. Had this fact anything to do with its choice as the legendary setting for the first telling of the Mahabharata? Did Vikramaditya regard the poem, perhaps, as a kind of Purana of India herself, as the national contribution to world-letters? Or are we to look for the explanation to the name Takshasila only (=Takshakasila?), and to the part played in the first volume by the great serpent Takshaka?

Supposing the year A.D. 400 to be rightly chosen as that of the final compilation of the Mahabharata, and the city of Pataliputra as the scene of its commissioning, it follows that the poem may be taken as an epitome of the Bengali civilisation of that period. We do not often realise how ample are the materials now in existence for a full and continuous narrative of Bengal. Sarat Chandra Das long ago pointed out that the city of Lhasa is a page taken out of mediæval Bengal. In the influence of the Bengali architect, Vidyadhar, in laying out the city of Jaipur in the reign of Sewai Jey Singh in the first half of the eighteenth century, we have evidence of a later date as to the greatness and enlightenment of the Bengali mind throughout its history. Those streets of Jaipur forty yards wide, that regard for air and the needs of sanitation, that marvellous development of the civic sense, are not modern and foreign but pre-English and Bengali in their source and origin. But to my own mind the Mahabharata is in this matter the master-document. Taking Vikramaditya as the reigning sovereign, we see here a people thoroughly conversant with civic and regal splendour. How beautiful and full of life is the following description of a city rejoicing :—

"And the citizens decorated the city with flags and standards and garlands of flowers. And the streets were watered and decked with wreaths and other ornaments. And at their gateways the citizens piled flowers. And their temples and shrines were all adorned with flowers."

There is need here, it should be added, of a

history of *books* in India. What were the first manuscripts of Mahabharata written on? When "the three Vedas" are referred to with such clearness and distinctness, how does the writer or speaker conceive of them? Is the picture in his mind that of a *book* or a *manuscript*; and if so of what composed? Or is it a choir of Brahmans, having as many parts and divisions as the Vedas themselves?

Behind all the exuberance of prosperity and happiness, moreover, in this poem, stands the life of reverence and earnest aspiration; the ideals of faith, purity, and courage, which pervade all classes of the people alike, and are the same to-day as they were under the empire of Pataliputra. As regards his ideal of learning, a young Bengali scholar of to-day belongs still to the culture of the Gupta period. A knowledge of Sanskrit from the ancient Vedic to the fashionable literary language of the day; an acquaintance with certain books; and the knowledge of a definite scheme of metaphysics, logic, and philosophy may be taken as the type of scholarship then. And very few are the Bengali minds that have yet reached a point in the assimilation and expression of a new form of thought and knowledge, which would make it possible to say that they are of another age than that of Vikramaditya. Of that new age Science is to be the pivot and centre, and there can be no doubt that the era of Science, with its collateral development of geography and history, will directly succeed that of the Guptas, with its Sanskrit literature and logic in Bengal. In order to pass from one type so highly evolved, however, into another which shall give the people an equal place in Humanity, it is necessary that the moral and ethical standards of the race shall grow, rather than relax, in strength and stability. The meeting line of periods is a time of winnowing and of judgment in the history of nations, and many are the souls to be scattered like chaff.

It is clear from many of the allusions in the life of Krishna, as told both in the Mahabharata and in the Puranas, that He directly, in most places, supersedes the Vedic gods. In the moment of his Ascension it is *Indra* who hymns Him. And already at Brindaban He has successfully preached the Law of Karma in opposition to Vedic sacrifice, and has succeeded in bringing Indra low in the ensuing contest. This new religion of Vishnu, indeed, like that of Shiva, belongs to a different class from that of the old nature-gods. The more modern are subjective. Their sphere is in the soul, and their power that of the highest ideals. Indra, Agni, Yama, and Varuna represented external forces, cosmic some of them, irresistible in their might by puny man, glorious, lovable, *but not of* THE WITHIN. They were supremely objective.

The story of Nala and Damayanti, coming as it does out of the earlier Vedic period, has nevertheless had its conclusion modified by the Gupta poets, in accordance with that amelioration of taste and manners which is inseparable from a great and long-established civilisation, and also doubtless with that high development of religious ideals which will always take place in India in periods of prosperity and power. We feel it artistically wrong that Koli (कलि) should be allowed to depart, and Pushkara should be forgiven. But the subjects of the Gupta emperors had been for ages accustomed to peace and wealth, and in the general refinement of the period reconciliation was desired as the dramatic climax, not revenge. The story of Savitri shows the same trend of popular taste in somewhat different fashion. She triumphs over death—not by the heroic methods of the earlier maiden, who could appeal to the honour of the gods and meet with jovial and thoroughly benevolent treatment in return, but by sheer force of the spiritual ideal. Born of prayer itself, prepared for the supreme encounter by vigil and fast, Savitri is no Vedic princess, but a tender, modern, Hindu woman. She belongs almost unconsciously to the coming era of subjective soul-staying faiths. The boisterous days of storm and fire and forest worships are now far behind.

Between these two ages, however, of the Vedic gods on the one hand, and the theological systems of Vishnu and Shiva on the other, there is in the Mahabharata and also in the Puraṇas to a less extent one anomalous figure. It is that of

Brahma the Creator, the benevolent four-headed Grandsire. Who was this Brahma? What is his exact significance? It might almost be stated as a law that in India there has never been a deity or a religious idea without some social formation behind it. What traces have we, then, of a Brahma-worshipping sect? At what period, and where, are we to look for it? Is there any connection between him and the story of Dattatreya? What is the history of his one temple and one image near Pushkar at Ajmir? Already, in the Mahabharata, He seems to be half-forgotten; yet if that work had been produced in the present age he would have received less mention still.

An important date to settle is that of Kalidas. If Chandragupta II of Pataliputra (A.D. 375 to 413) be really the famous Vikramaditya of Ujjain, it is difficult to see how Kalidas can have been one of the jewels of his court. Hinduism would seem first to have formulated the idea of Shiva, then that of Vishnu (as Lakshmi-Narayana), next that of Rama, and lastly that of Krishna. Between the theological conception of Lakshmi-Narayana and the concreted conception of Rama, Kalidas appears to have lived. His imagination was greatly touched by the conception of the Trinity, which must have been newly completed in his time. Personally he was overshadowed by the idea of Shiva, and he was not without foresight of the deification of Rama. Hindu scholars should be able from these considerations to fix his date.

The glimpses which the Mahabharata every now and again affords us of the worship ot Surya, or the sun, would suggest this rather as a royal than as a popular devotion. And the hypothesis is more or less borne out by the traces of his worship which remain in various parts of India. In Kashmir, in Orissa, and here and there in unexpected places, we meet with architectural and sculptural remains of it. But amongst the people it seems to have left few or no traces. Surya is counted academically amongst the Five Manifestations of the Supreme Being according to Hinduism, but devotionally, of what account is He?

These are questions that call for study and reply. Personally I believe that as our understanding of India progresses, we shall more and more be led to recognise the importance of place and history in accounting for those differentiations which certain common ideas have gradually undergone. It has not been opposition of opinion, but mere diversity of situation, which has been the source of the existing variety of sects and schools.

THE RISE OF VAISHNAVISM UNDER THE GUPTAS

THERE have been many Vaishnavisms, and any adequate history of the subject must make some attempt to take account of them all. Let us begin at the end, with the movement of Chaitanya in the fifteenth century. This would seem to have swept over Bengal like a fever. Wherever it went, it conquered high and low alike. It availed itself of the severest learning, and yet penetrated at the same time to the hearts of the most ignorant. It embraced and transformed all that was left of Buddhism. It established Brindaban as a great college of piety, holiest of *tirthas*, and most notable of *ashramas*. It ended outside Bengal by creating a new order of architecture, and inside her boundaries by forging a great vernacular on its anvil. And yet in the form given to it by Chaitanya and Nityananda it was a Bengali rather than an all-India movement. It centred in Radha and Krishna and the story of the Gopis. The contemporary movement in the rest of India selected for emphasis now this element, now that, in the older Vaishnavism. Here it anchored itself on Sita and Rama; there it found and clung to some other rock. It ended by placing Lakshmi-Narayana on the altar of worship. It is Lakshmi-Narayana who is worshipped throughout Maharashtra and Gujarat. It is Lakshmi-Narayana that we find at Badri Narayan, in the valleys of that diocese. The older Satya-Narayana had disputed with Shiva the possession of the road from Hardwar to Kedar Nath, but it was the latest wave, the mediæval revival, that captured the pilgrimage from Srinagar to Badri.

Had there been a Lakshmi in the older Vaishnavism? If not, what determined her inclusion in this mediæval renascence? A thousand years of social history lie in the answer to this question. It is an answer that can only be made definite by a detailed study of the different sects and orders of modern Vaishnavism, and a comparison of their beliefs, customs, and traditions. In this land of religious conservation, we may rely upon it that the whole story of its own development is written upon the brow of the faith itself, for the first trained eyes to decipher. We may depend upon it also, that each phase and form of the central idea has had its own individual history, most likely preserved in it as an essential tradition. Nothing that survived has occurred by accident; nothing has been created out of wantonness, or out of an idle desire to be different from others. Ideas so born must at once have perished. The synthesis of Vaishnavism to-day is what it has been made by its own history.

One thing is somewhat puzzling. Why was the

devotion of the Rajputani Meera Bai of so Bengali a type? It is the love of Krishna with which she is enrapt. It is Brindaban towards which all her wanderings tend. There was some strong and special bond during the Middle Ages that knit together Rajputana and Bengal. This is shown in the anxiety of Rajput princes for the recovery of Gaya from the Mussalmans. No history of Vaishnavism can be complete if it does not, on the one hand, account for its own differences as between Bengal and other provinces; and, on the other, explain the Chaitanya-like personality of Meera Bai.

To the Indian consciousness, this mediæval renascence was bound up with a strong movement for the assertion of the rights of Woman as well as of the People. That the religious faculty of humanity is as much feminine as masculine; that woman has as much right as man to abandon the career of the household for the life of the soul—these are amongst the convictions that throned Lakshmi beside Narayana during this period as the centre of Vaishnavite worship. It may be, further, that they are part of the inheritance taken over by it from Buddhism. The thirteen hundred women and twelve hundred men who were received into the congregation by Nityananda, at Khardaha, cannot have been altogether without precedent or parallel. Nor can they, with all their wretchedness, have failed to hold a strong conviction of the equal right of woman with man to play a part in the life of religion. And if it be true that they represented an old Buddhistic order, bewildered by its oblivion of its own history, puzzled by the absence of a niche for it in the Hindu synthesis it saw about it, then it follows that this idea of the religious right of woman was of old and deep growth in the Indian mind.

Mediæval Vaishnavism seems to have had its origin in the South, in the great teachers Ramanuja and Madhavacharya. In the Himalayas it has made a notable renewal of the relations of North and South. Both Kedar Nath and Badri Narayan must take their *mahants* or *raouls* from Madras, and though this rule may have begun with Sankaracharya, it must have been revitalised later. On the Vaishnava altars of the *Dravida-desh* itself, as also at Gaya, Narayana reigns for the most part alone. That is to say, He dates from an older than the Badri Narayan or Maharashtra stratum of Vaishnava doctrine. And this is right. It is in the missionary-country that the propaganda of a given moment finds its fullest scope. Thus Buddhism, which is only a single phase of Hinduism, becomes a national religion in Burma and Ceylon. It remains but one element in a great matrix in the land of its birth. It is to the South then that we must go if we would learn of the older Vaishnavism. It is its religious organisation and its temple-ritual that we must study, if we would know what was the background from which sprang Ramanuja, or what was the heaven for which the mother of

Sankaracharya yearned, if indeed the exquisite story of her death-bed be not a later Vaishnavite gloss.

Southern Vaishnavism is the Vaishnavism of the Gupta empire. It was the Vaishnavism that was spread far and wide with the story of the Mahabharata. The *Pandava-Lila* of the Southern villages, and the Pandava legends of the Northern *tirtha* have a single chronological origin. They both alike belong to the culture that was promulgated during the fourth, fifth, and sixth centuries under the later Pataliputra Empire. Only in the South do we find temples in which the image of Krishna is worshipped as Partha-Sarathi, the charioteer of Arjuna, because only in the South does the Gupta influence remain to this day in its purity and strength. The Narayana image of the South now is the old Narayana—Satya-Narayana, as he was called—of Magadha. It is the same Narayana that was placed by Skanda Gupta on the top of the Bhitari Lat about A.D. 460, when he set this up with the double purpose of commemorating his father's *sraddha* and his own victory over the Huns. It is the same Narayana that seems to have been carved so freely in Bengal under the Pal dynasty, after Gour became the capital.

"As Krishna hastened to Devaki," says the priceless inscription on the Bhitari Lat, with the news of his victory over his enemies, so went Skanda Gupta to his mother.

Twice in the national epic itself Krishna is addressed by such titles as "Slayer of Putana," showing, as does this inscription, that Mahabharata Vaishnavism, though mainly dependent for its central figure on the Krishna of the *Bhagavat Gita*, was intended to include and confirm the story of Gokul and Mathura. How much of Brindaban episode there may have been in this original nucleus of the great tale it is for the critics of language and literature to determine. The relative ages of the *Harivansa*, *Vishnu* and *Bhagat Purana* hold that secret between them. That the child Krishna was always the slayer of demons we may be quite sure. This aspect was of his very essence. Are divine beings not always known by their slaying of demons? It is only when the fact of their divinity is firmly established in our minds that our attention can be claimed for their Gospels and their *Gitas*.

In an age of great education and general understanding of the essentials of the Faith, the throne of Pataliputra had to show that the older Saivism was not the only form of religion that could ratify and popularise the sublime truths of the Upanishads. The Babe who had dwelt amongst the cowherds on the Jumna-side had nevertheless been of royal Hindu parentage, and it was told of him that when the usurper had been slain, He was at once sent away by Devaki and Vasudeva to be instructed in the Vedas.[1] Thus the Grand Personality, that towers above Kurukshetra and enunciates the body of doctrine which all India in

[1] See *Vishnu*, *Harivansa*, and *Bhagavat Puranas*.

the year A.D. 400 knew to be the core of *dharma*, combines in himself the divinity of the Indian Shiva, the virility of the Greek Herakles, the simplicity of the Judæan Christ, the tenderness of Buddha, and the calm austerity and learning of any teacher of the Upanishads. The great truths He utters were in the very air during the period when the Mahabharata was put into its present form under the patronage of the Guptas of Pataliputra. It was essential that the Divine Incarnation should give voice to the whole scheme of personal discipline and salvation, and that utterance forms in the present case the *Bhagavad Gita*. The potential power that formed the background of the new faith is seen in the fact that the presence of *Salagrama*, as the symbol of Vishnu, has been essential ever since to the legality of a Hindu marriage.

The tide of this Gupta Vaishnavism lifted and reinterpreted many already familiar elements of life. The image of Narayana that it made its own, was a natural development from the figure that the sculptors were at that time in the habit of cutting on the stupas. The three little earthen mounds, placed side by side, that the common people were so apt then as now to make for adoration, were explained by the new movement as a symbol of Jaganath, Lord of the Universe. It gave a like account of the prevalent worship of a sacred footprint. It incorporated Buddha Deva in its own synthesis, as undoubtedly the tenth incarnation of

Vishnu. It accepted and perpetuated the sanctity of Brahma-Gaya, as distinguished from Bodh-Gaya. And there and at other well-known *tirthas* of that period it endorsed the complex customs that have grown up—probably under the influence of Chinese and Tibetan pilgrims and merchants—of prayer for the dead.

Nor need we suppose that when the Mahabharata was first promulgated, Krishna shone so much alone as He seems to us to do to-day. To us the whole tangle of culture that bears the name of the Mahabharata appears largely as a setting for the *Bhagavad Gita*. But on its first publication, it was almost equally impressive in all its parts. Bhishma and Karna and each of the Pandavas, had his place and his glory in the national imagination. Nay, a complete map of the shrines and altars in Garhwal would show that even the poets who contributed fragments—as well as Vyasa, welder of the vast composition into a whole—were held worthy of special honour and enthusiasm.

Thus was established Vaishnavism, as woof upon the warp of Indian religion for the time to come. What was Shiva, we wonder, in the minds of those who knelt so eagerly at this period before the Incarnation of Vishnu? Was He merely Nagesvar or Nilkanta? Had He yet become Ardha-nari? Probably not; for if He had, it is difficult to see how He could have been superseded by Satya-Narayana, without Lakshmi, as was probably the case.

In this question of religious ideas that formed the firmament in which Krishna rose we have a fruitful field of study. A great deal can be inferred from the stories that have gathered round the name of the divine cowherd. Brahma tests Him, to see if He is in truth an incarnation of Vishnu. Here the idea of Brahma as the creator has evidently not yet been supplanted amongst the Aryan classes, and yet the doctrine of the Trinity is implicit, for Brahma shows the assumption that Vishnu is His own equal. Krishna conquers the snake Kaliya, and leaves His own footprint on his head. Here is the same struggle that we can trace in the personality of Shiva as Nageswara between the new devotional faith and the old traditional worship of snakes and serpents. He persuades the shepherds to abandon the sacrifice to Indra. Here He directly overrides the older Vedic gods, who, as in some parts of the Himalayas to-day, seem to know nothing of the interposition of Brahma. And throughout the Mahabharata Shiva gives testimony to the divinity of Krishna, but Krishna never says a word about that of Shiva! That is to say, the divinity of Shiva was well known, was taken for granted, by both poet and audience, but that of Krishna had yet to be established. We shall find that in the ritual of the South the religious procession forms as important a feature as it must have been in the Buddhist *chaityas*. Here we read of authoritative organisation in a period when such spectacles had powerfully impressed the pious imagination.

It would appear therefore that a great formative movement took place in the history of Vaishnavism when India was potentially united under the Guptas, and when Buddhism had become so highly developed and over-ripe that the story of its origin was losing definiteness in the popular mind. This epoch saw the synthesis, under indisputable suzerain authority, of the doctrinal Krishna, Partha-Sarathi, speaker of the *Gita,* and the popular Krishna, the Gopala of Gokool, and Hero of Mathura. The same period saw missions despatched to the South for the preaching of this great consolidated faith, and the parcelling out of Garhwal and Kumaon, in the Himalayas, as pre-eminently the land of the Pandava *tirthas.* This consolidation of the story and idea of Krishna was in all probability connected with the last recension of the Mahabharata, which was probably in its turn the work of an official synod of poets under Samudra Gupta and Chandra Gupta II, Vikramaditya, between A.D. 330 and 455. We know for a fact that the succeeding Guptas were devoted worshippers of Narayana in His incarnation as Krishna, and that in this worship Krishna the son of Devaki, and Krishna the slayer of Kansa, were joined.

Not yet however have we exhausted the story of Indian Vaishnavism. Even before the rise of Saivism there had been a still older worship of Vishnu. When the idea of the Trinity came in, with the idea of the exaltation of Shiva, Vishnu was at once made its Second Person. In all lists of the gods—Ganesha, Surya, Indra, Brahma or Agni, Vishnu, Shiva and Durga—He is named before Shiva. In this fact there must be history. Out of that history came the centuries of Vaishnavism which, in consolidated Hinduism of the ages succeeding Sankaracharya, formed one of the two strands of which the rope of the national faith was twisted. From the time of the early Buddhism onwards we may watch the growth of an organised Indian faith in which Saivism and Vaishnavism are oscillating phases. A century of silence means only some episode to be recovered and recorded. Numberless must be the links between Sankaracharya and Chaitanya; for it is part and parcel of the nature of things that the Hindu development shall proceed by a regular alternation from Saivism to Vaishnavism and Vaishnavism to Saivism, and that the epoch-maker, the Avatar, shall be born again and again.

THE HISTORICAL SIGNIFICANCE OF THE NORTHERN PILGRIMAGE

A Brief Summary of the Sequence of Hinduism as seen in the Himalayas

Buddhism and prehistoric Hinduism, largely planetary, worship of Daksha, Ganesh, Garud, Narasinha, &c.

Hindu Shiva—in succession to Brahma—the four-headed Shivas at Gopeswar, the four-headed Dharma-chakra at Agastyamuni and at Joshi Math.

Era of Devi-worship—Synthetising itself to Siva, with Ganesha as son. Nine forms of Devi, Kedar Nath, Joshi Math, Shiva and Parbati. Later, Shiva becomes Ardhanari the Shiva in three stages, and as at Gupta Kashi, also Gopeswar, also Devi Dhura, above Kathgodam, also Kamaleswar in Srinagar.

Possible Era of the Ramayana—Dronprayag and all places named on behalf of Rama, &c.

Era of the Mahabharata, bringing in worship of Satya Narayana. Traces numerous, Vyasa Ganga to Kedar Nath, &c.

Temple of five Pandavas, before entering Srinagar.

Sankaracharyan Shiva-worship. Bilwakedar, Kedar Nath, Bhethu Chati.

Mediæval Vaishnavism. Srinagar, Gupta Kashi, Bhethu Chati, Kedar Nath, and the valleys of Badri Narayana.

Shiva again substituted for Narayana at Gupta Kashi under pressure of some special circumstances.

It must be understood that each of these phases is liable to develop itself continuously from its inception, so that none of the succeeding eras stand alone. At each place named, it may be only a trace that is left of any given era. It must not be expected that the site shall be eloquent of it.

THE great places of pilgrimage, Kedar Nath and Badri Narayana, in the Himalayas, are to be regarded as the cathedral cities of adjacent dioceses. Each has its four dependent centres, and the still smaller diocese of Gopeswar has also its minor sites of religious importance. On the road to Gangotri there is an old religious capital called Barahat; and Adi Badri must not be forgotten—on the road to Kathgodam. By all, the visit of Sankaracharya—sometime between A.D. 600 and 800—is claimed as if it had been a recent event, vividly remembered; and this would tend, other things being conformable, to show that these sites were already old at the time of his coming. We can hardly doubt that this was so. It is evident enough that in his name a strong wave of Saivism swept up all the valleys of the Himalayas. It is this wave, the work of this gigantic epoch-making mind, that finally purged the Saivite idea of all its prehistoric physical elements, and fastened upon Shiva the subtle poetic conception of the great monk, throned on the snows and lost in one eternal meditation. Everything in Hindu imagery of Mahadeva that conflicts with this notion is pre-Sankaracharyan.

Even in this, however, it must be remembered that Sankaracharya is rather the end of a process than an individual. In the *Kumara Sambhava*, the Birth of the War Lord, of Kalidasa, we see the same

Aryanizing process at work on the congeries of elements that even then were seething and fuming about the feet of one who would fain cast himself upon the ocean of the thought of God as Shiva. A people that had learnt under Buddhism to worship the solitary life of spiritual culture, a people whose every instinct made for the sanctity of the home and the purity of the family, found themselves on the one hand enwrapt by the conception of God as the Great Monk, and on the other puzzled by the presence of Parbati with a train of alien associations. The riddle was solved by the genius of Kalidasa. In the *Kumara Sambhava* he vindicated triumphantly the Indian ideal of woman and marriage. In Uma we have a vision of life and love in which the Aryan imagination can rest without tremor or misgiving. The last remnant of early Bacchus-ideals is banished, however, by the stern fiat of Sankaracharya. Even the popular imagination is called into leash. The Great God is established finally as the light of knowledge within the soul, Purusha the stirless, the Destroyer of Ignorance. The great prayer to Rudra:

> From the Unreal lead us to the Real!
> From Darkness lead us unto Light!
> From Death lead us to Immortality!
> Reach us through and through ourself
> And evermore protect us—Oh Thou Terrible!—
> from ignorance,
> By Thy Sweet Compassionate Face!

might well have been the utterance of Sankaracharya

in the hour of placing the keystone in the arch of the national conception.

The emblem of Shiva which was established by the teacher for worship, in supersession of all others, would seem to have been the hump or heap of natural rock, as we find it at Kedar Nath, at the Kedar Nath monastery in Benares, at Bilwakedar, and elsewhere. I found it recently in a temple on the Ganges bank above Dakkhineswar. The emblem that had been in use before his time was undoubtedly that in three stages—cube, octagonal cylinder, and thimble-shaped top—the form which was universal in the time of Varahamihira, A.D. 550.

But this Shiva was too intimately associated with the image of Ardha-nari, even as we find it at Gupta Kashi, to be tolerable to the fastidious mind of Sankaracharya. He would have no Shiva in the midst of his Saktis—the interpretation which had now transformed the four-headed Brahma into the Tantrik Mahadeva, as at Gopeswar, and at Chandra Nath near Chittagong.

Nor would he have a form even remotely capable of a phallic rendering. To this fiery monastic intelligence such a significance was in itself degradation. Back, then, to the ancient sanctity of the mound, back to the purity and simplicity of nature! By a curious irony of history, the violent enemy of Buddhist Tantrik abuses became the restorer of the Buddhist stupa to worship! The taste of the whole people endorsed his criticism, and, even as they seem to have accepted his repudiation of human sacrifice in the cause of Mother-worship at Srinagar, so at each sacred site they set up the Great God for supreme veneration, and where this deity was new they established Him in his Sankaracharyan form. At Gupta Kashi, whatever its name then was, Shiva was already worshipped as Ardha-nari, and no change was made, though we cannot doubt that the spiritual impact of the new thought was adequately realised. But at Kedar Nath itself, and at Bhethu Chati, where Satya-Narayana, or Vishnu was the chief deity, Shiva in his new form was substituted.

The same tide of the Sankaracharyan energy swept also over the valleys leading up to Badri Narayan, and Joshi Math and Pipal-koti still remain to testify to the pre-Ramanuja Saivism of these parts. But at Joshi Math there are traces in abundance of a world still older than that of Sankaracharya. Its theological name—Dhyani Badri—suggests to the ear that *Badri* is a corruption of *Buddha*, and opens up a long vista of antiquity. Whether this be so or not, its position on the Tibetan road has exposed it to a whole series of influences from which the more secluded valleys of Kedar Nath have been protected. By comparing the two, we may perhaps succeed in computing the number and importance of the Mongolian elements that have entered into the great synthesis called Hinduism.

The true place of Badri Narayan in history may perhaps be better understood when it is mentioned that it was long a pilgrimage of obligation to the Tibetan lamas, and that even now certain Tibetan monasteries pay it tribute. It is for them, in fact, the first of that chain of sacred places that ends for the Buddhistic nations with Gaya. Seen from this point of view the importance of Badri Narayana as a place of *sraddh* acquires a new significance. It is the holiest of all. The requiem that has been said here may be repeated nowhere else. The dead whose repose has here been prayed for reach final peace. It will, I think, be found that there is no special place of *sraddh* in India which is not either a place of Buddhistic pilgrimage, or else, like Deva Prayag, an important point on the Tibetan road. And while the habit of prayer for and benediction of the dead is one to which the human heart everywhere must respond, there is not an equal universality, perhaps, in the mode of thought that regards as somehow spoilt and exhausted, the rice, furnishings, and money that are dedicated as oblations to the departed. There is in this an element curiously incongruous with our modern Indo-European modes of feeling, though it has much that is kindred to it in ancient Egyptian and in the Chinese faith. Yet the poetry of the prayer that can be perfected only on the sunlit heights of Badri Narayan none will, I think, gainsay. Here sorrow ends in peace. Here the dead parent and the living child are uplifted together in a common soothing. And the Love of God throbs out, like a lighted lamp within the shrine, across that temple-court, where the women perform *pradakshina*, telling their beads and lost in the dream beyond life and death alike.

The mediæval Vaishnavism that began with Ramanuja and dominated the whole life of India in so many ways during the Middle Ages, captured Badri Narayan and its subject seats. But at Kedar Nath it only succeeded in establishing the minor pilgrimage of Triyugi Narayana in the immediate neighbourhood. The name of this shrine marks the same eager ambition as is found in the legend of Narada at the temple of the five Pandavas in Srinagar, to claim for itself continuity with an older pre-Sankaracharyan orthodox authentic Hinduism. This was the same Vaishnavism that blossomed later into the Ramayana of Tulsi Das. It was the same that found expression in Guru Nanak in the Punjab, in Tukaram in Maharashtra, and even—though in such different form—in Chaitanya in Bengal. Alike in the life of Ramanuja, in Chaitanya, in Guru Nanak, and in Tukaram, it is pre-eminently an uprising of the people. In Meera Bai in Rajputana it represents opportunity for women, and in the Himalayas at least it found expression in a new order of architecture, seen in perfection at Bhethu Chati—the tall lily-like tower crowned with the *amalaki*, which is slightly more modern than the great temple of Bhubaneswar in Orissa, even as that represents a later phase of the

Bodh-Gaya type. One of the most interesting problems of Indian history lies in the question why a movement that was marked by so many common features throughout the rest of India should have assumed so distinctive a character in Bengal. Vaishnavism as a whole is a subject that calls for careful and extensive study. Its history will be found to be twisted out of many strands, and it will often happen that some slight disagreement on a point of doctrine or symbolism indicates a difference of ages and of provinces in origin. Going back to the period before the Saivism of Sankaracharya and before even the Satya-Narayana that it superseded, what do we find, of an older Hinduism still? There can be no doubt that the Ramachandra of Deva-Prayag is older. Here Ramachandra would seem to have been established before the time of the Guptas (A.D. 319 onwards) when Shiva was the chief deity of Hinduism. Just as in the Ramayana itself, so also here at Deva-Prayag, the one statement made and emphasized is that Rama the Incarnation of Vishnu *is* Shiva. That is to say, the Godhead of Shiva, when this site was dedicated, was nowhere in dispute. It was not a point that called for argument. We cannot help wondering if there was not an early attempt to *Ramayanise* the whole Himavant, so to say. Lakshman Jhula met us at the very outset of our journey. And it is certain that "the days of Rama" seem antiquity itself to the people, and that every village not otherwise named is Rampur or Rambarra or Ramnagar.

Whether this was so or not, it is fairly certain that in the age when a knowledge of the Mahabharata represented ideal culture, a great and authoritative effort was made to associate this whole region with the Pandavas. That the attempt was undertaken with an eye to the work as literature, and not on the basis of prehistoric traditions, is shown by the little chapel dedicated to Vyasa, in the valley of Vyasaganga. Here the pilgrim about to follow up the stations of the Mahabharata could first make salutation to the master-poet. Of all the elements contained in this particular stratum of tradition, the personality of Bhima—or, as the people call him, "Bhim Sen"—the strong man of Hinduism, stands out as most prehistoric. There is here something unique, something that has a sanction of its own in the popular mind not derived from its place in the national epic.

If there really was a prior movement for connecting Himavant with the ideas of the Ramayana, succeeded by the Mahabharata-epoch—bringing in the worship of Satya-Narayana—then before either of these came the great era of Devi. There is a chapel of the nine forms of Devi still at Kedar Nath, and the oldest and most active of the seven minor temples at Joshi Math contains the same images. In order really to understand this idea, it would be necessary to make a separate and complete study of it, as it is found in all the different parts of India. But in the meantime it is fairly certain that in its most elaborate form it made its advent into these mountains before the era of Satya-Narayana, and it is worth while also to note the relationship of its great centres to the Tibetan road. Two of these are Gopeswar, and Devi Dhura.

The impulse of Devi-worship seems to have been synthetizing. It attached itself to that cult of Shiva which was already accepted and, carrying with it the prehistoric Ganesha, established a holy family. No one who has heard the tale of the headless Ganesha below Kedar Nath can fail to recognise the fact that this god had already had a history, before being established as the son of Shiva and Parbati. The frequency of his images is one of the surest marks of age in a Shiva-shrine, and his medallion over the door of the chaitya-shaped building that covers the spring at Bhethu Chati, marks out that structure, as surely as does its Buddhistic form, for the oldest of the buildings in the neighbourhood.

Before any of these developments there came the Buddhistic missionaries, who from the time of the great Nirvana, carried the Gospel to the Himavant. Of this phase of history little or no trace remains, save in the chaitya-form of the shrine of the Mother at Gopeswar, the spring-cover at Bhethu Chati, and the temple of the nine forms of Devi at Joshi Math, and in the fact that at Nalla we see the development of the temple out of the stupa. Whether besides this the very word "Badri"—with its "Dhyani Badri" as the esoteric name of

Joshi Math—is also a trace of Buddhism must be decided by others. One thing is clear. All the Buddhistic texts and deeds that are written on birch-bark come from the Himalayas, and as these are many, the Himalayas must have been the scene of great life and activity during the Buddhistic period.

The whole region of the pilgrimage, even better than that of Orissa, forms a *cul-de-sac* of Hinduism in which one may study the birth and origin of manifold things that have gone to form the great synthesis of the national faith. The sensitiveness that certain sites have shown to the whole historic sequence of religious developments marks their early establishment as Buddhistic centres. And in every case we find the characteristic that distinguishes the Hindu temple still, the tendency to gather round the central theme or shrine an account of the religion as it stands at the moment. The tendency to crowd on a single site temple, stupa, sacred tree, school, monastery, and *dharmsala* is one that may be seen in Buddhist countries still, throwing a flood of light on the genesis of such places as Agastyamuni, Kamaleswar, Nalla, and Gopeswar.

The northern *tirtha* forms a great palimpsest of the history of Hinduism. Record has here been written upon record. Wave has succeeded wave. And still the bond that knits these farthest points north to the farthest south is living and unbroken, and the people stream along the pilgrim roads in worship, to testify to the fact that without the conception of India as a whole we can explain no single part or item of the Indian life. But the greatest of all syntheses is that which is written in the minds and hearts of the simple Himalayan peasantry themselves. Successive waves of sectarian enthusiasm have made their country what it is, but the people themselves are no sectaries. To them Shiva, Devi, and Narayan are all sacred, and in their grasp of the higher philosophy of Hinduism they are without exception true Hindus.

THE OLD BRAHMANICAL LEARNING

In following up the history of any one of the Indian vernacular literatures, one is likely to be struck with the fact that they take their subjects for the most part from somewhere else, from something outside themselves. They are organs of response, not altogether seats of creativeness; they give expression to something which they have first received. There is of course a layer of vernacular literature—socially the most rustic and plebeian—which is the repository of the tastes of the people. Here the common motives of popular romance—love, hate, desertion, fortune, reunion, the favours of supernatural beings, the temporary triumph of the wicked, the unmerited sufferings of the good, and the "all happy ever after"—have free play, as in all countries and all ages. Even this stratum however in its main undulations, betrays the tastes that are characteristic of the higher walks of vernacular literature during the passing period. Persecuted beauty is made to go through the fiery ordeal by more or less far-fetched doubts cast upon its virtue, when Sita happens to be the popular ideal; and manly strength is put to tests that bring it into line with the fashionable heroes of the hour. Waves of influence seem to pass across the ocean of democratic poetry in each succeeding period, moulding its surface with less and less distinctness as the level of formal education sinks, but assuredly determining its main heights and descents.

What is the character of these influences? What is their central source of stimulus? What is that brain to which the literatures of the various provinces act as limbs and organs? Is there any mainspring from which all alike draw simultaneous inspiration? And if so, what is it, and where are we to look for it?

Such a fountain of energy and direction does certainly exist, guiding and colouring the whole intellectual life of the Indian people from generation to generation. It is found in the ancient Sanskrit learning of the Brahman caste. Here is that floating university and national academy of letters of which the various vernacular languages form as it were so many separate colleges. Here we can watch a single unresting course of evolution, and see it reflected at a certain interval of time, with a certain variety and tremulousness of outlines, in the poetry and letters of each of the provincial peoples.

The great national epics, the Mahabharata and Ramayana, are in Sanskrit, and stand to this day as the type and standard of imaginative culture amongst all save the English-educated classes.

The story is learned, and the personalities become familiar through village-plays and grandmothers' tales, and the constant reference of everyone about one from childhood upwards. But *quotation* can only be made from the Sanskrit, and, with the beautiful precision of mediæval learning, must be accompanied by careful word-by-word translation into the vulgar tongue. This is the rule, whatever the caste of the speaker, though naturally enough we hear such references oftener from the lips of a Brahman than from any other.

The translation of either of the epics into one of the minor languages usually marks a literary epoch. It is never a close or exact rendering. The translator allows himself as much liberty as Shakespeare in dealing with English history; and a very interesting comparative study of the ideals of different provinces might be made on the basis of the six or seven great names that could be chosen from among the authors of these variants. Tulsi Das, the writer of the Hindi Ramayana of the fifteenth century, is one of the springs and fountains of life to the people of the North-West Provinces; as indeed to all the Vaishnavas of Northern India. He regarded himself as only a reciter or interpreter of the great work of Valmiki, but he has carried out his task in such a fashion as himself to hold the rank of a great original poet.

Yet the Mahabharata and Ramayana, with the long succeeding train of Sanskrit poetry, do not themselves form the subject of that severe Brahmanical training which was the backbone of the old Indian culture. The supreme wisdom of the system is seen nowhere better than in the fact that poetry and the fruits of imagination are allowed to go free. Metre and the rules of prosody are studied in connection with grammar and Vedic enunciation, but the national sagas are regarded as more or less popular and easy, and left to the private reading of the student or to the more serious labours of professional minstrels, bards, and wandering tale-tellers. What an interesting inquiry might be carried out in India, as to the relative numbers of works of literary genius which emanate from the ranks of professional and amateur writers respectively! At any rate, it was not the epics themselves, but that world of thought and philosophy out of which they were born, that environment which presses upon and utters itself even now through both teller and hearers—it was this whose fires were kept so vigorously alight by the Brahmanical organisation of scholarship.

We do not sufficiently realise the fact that mediæval Hindu India was organised round universities, instead of round political centres. Vikrampore, Nuddea, and Mithila were the master-names of Bengali life and thought ever after the downfall of Gour and Rungpur as capital-cities. Dacca and Murshidabad were centres of administration and finance. But for the sources of their intellectual and spiritual energies men looked to the seats of Sanskritic learning, not to the thrones of the Nawabs. Even Mohammedanism in its turn had to create its own centres of scholarship, and with its instinct for seizing on the elaborated achievements of Buddhism, it took Jaunpur, which remains to-day as the fount of episcopal authority for Islamic India. Vikrampur with its long Buddhistic history had enjoyed an intervening period of importance as the capital of the Sens, or there might have been a like ambition to claim its prestige also for the foreign scheme of culture. We must not too hastily assume that this would have been a loss. The world has seen few types of courtly accomplishment and bearing so fine as that of the scholars in whom a knowledge of Persian was added to the ordinary training in Sanskrit. It was essentially a system of cultivation destined to turn out a man-of-the-world, and thereby how different from the severe depth and austerity of the Brahmanic ideal! But it was very beautiful and delightful in its own way. The Persian education of the old *maulvis* of Jaunpur gave a most finished appreciation of great literature. The Islamic scholar and Sanskrit pundit had this in common, that they were both mediævalists, both devoted students of high poetry, both thankful to be poor if only thereby they might be, wise, and both accustomed to spend a dozen years over a single book. It was the bone and marrow of the poem on which their hearts were set, and they often bred up a race of students in whom taste was unerring. Never have I seen the sense of literature so developed as in a certain Hindu monk, who in his childhood had learned Persian from an old scholar in Jaunpur. Mankind will be tangibly poorer when a few grey-headed men who live about Benares, Patna, and Lucknow, shall have passed away, and their sons, stepping into their vacant places, prove to be of a newer breed.

The Hindu universities of the past were distinguished each to some extent by its own specialism. Thus the South was great for the recitation of the Vedas. Even now, in the great temple of Conjeeveram one may imagine oneself in ancient Egypt, as one listens, in the early morning hours, to the fresh young voices of the choir-school in the distance reciting the ancient texts. And the whole of southern society assists in the concentration necessary to this task, for it is required that even laymen listening to the *rijks* (stanzas) shall, at the first sound of a letter or a syllable misplaced, manifest violent disgust and distress. This may not seem like good manners, but it is most eloquent of the accuracy demanded in repetition. Similarly, Nuddea in Bengal was noted for its logic. Here again, as in literature, the highest fruit grows in freedom. Nasik and Punderpur in Maharashtra had each its own strong point. And for all—grammar, philosophy, and texts—the crown was Benares. Nor can the pre-eminence of the divine city be said even yet to have departed. There still are the great libraries with the scholars that pore over their treasures and compare texts day after day.

There are the laborious schools of the pundits, with their pupils committing verses to heart in sing-song through the hottest hours. There are the grave and reverend professors of the highest ideas of the ancient wisdom, only too glad to lay open their treasures to any who will forsake all to follow truth. Still the poor scholars tramp their way here from all over India. Still on winter mornings one may come upon the student up before dawn, reading aloud to himself in the bleak shelter of some corner. He will go on doing this for twelve years at least, before he will be declared to have a knowledge of his book, and be fit to use his knowledge in the world outside. But by that time he will have the root of the matter in him, and the temptations of luxury and idleness will have ceased to speak to him.

But it is for the most part in the small country *tolls* in remote places, like Vikrampur with its hundred villages, that the Brahmanic learning is built up. ,Here the great problem of the education and initiation of the comparatively young and unlearned into the path of higher inquiry is solved. When a student arrives at a *toll* he is already of a certain age, which may be anything from fifteen to twenty-five. The only children there are the sons and daughters, the nieces and nephews, of the *guru* or master. From old men who were children of the family in these Sanskrit colleges we may still glean what we desire to know about the life there, for a commercial age has shattered the old learning and with it the system of institutions by which it was imparted. Men have not now that large sweet leisure, or that freedom from anxiety, which characterised the old times. Everything has now had its money value measured and assigned, and there is scarcely enough to fill the hungry mouths. A family cannot dispense with the services of one member who might be an earner. Learning did not necessarily in the old times make a man poor, for he might rise through it to great distinction and emolument. But it provided him with so many claims that it left him poor in the end, whatever it may have made him in the beginning. The students who arrived at the *toll* paid nothing for the instructions which they received. It was sufficient that they were content to give their lives and labour. Their master was the treasurer of wisdom as well as her exponent. He found the means. There would sometimes be as many as a hundred scholars in a single *toll*, and so great was the fame of Bengal for logic that men would come from the most remote part of the country to join the training of a certain teacher. Intercourse could always be carried on in a *toll* in Sanskrit. In one of these rustic colleges in distant Vikrampur, I have heard of two Mahratta students. Customs were made a little elastic to give the necessary margin to the two strangers, but they lived with their Bengali *guru* and brethren for many a long year, and departed at last to carry their name and fame far and wide.

A man on his arrival, begging the *guru* to take him as a disciple, was supposed to be already interested in some special line of study. He was then set to learn a given book. This had to be committed to memory, and also thoroughly digested and understood. The hearing of the recitation each morning included also a searching examination into matter and criticism. If the result were not satisfactory, the hint was given by suggestion that it should be re-read, and then a visit would be paid by the master privately during the reading for special exposition and assistance, as soon as the other recitations had been heard.

The next stage in the day's work consisted of the lecture, when a new portion of the treatise that was being studied was taken in hand and expounded by the pundit. Such were the pursuits that occupied the hours of the morning and early afternoon. The glory and delight of college-life came towards evening, when the shadows began to grow, and formal work was over for the day. Then teacher and students together would set out for the afternoon walk. Across the fields they would proceed, in twos and threes, earnestly discussing the questions which had arisen in the course of their studies. Perhaps they would end by paying a friendly visit to another *toll* in some neighbouring village. Or perhaps they would return home to find a bevy of visitors come to discuss with them. In deep disputation the evening would pass, food unthought of. And it was no unheard-of thing that the guests should lie down at some late hour and stay the night, in order to rise up next morning and renew the fray.

It was in these discussions that the originality and powers of the students were really developed. They also show how essential it was that one *toll* should be situated in a district where there were others. Sometimes the argument would assume excitement and almost the dimensions of a pitched battle. We feel this when we read the wonderful story of Chaitanya, who was at first a scholar of Nuddea. There came to him in his days of Sanskrit scholarship a pundit from Benares, determined to worst him, famous as he was, in argument. The battle was felt to be the cause of Nuddea against Benares, and sympathy was naturally quick for the home of the listeners. On the other hand the age and distinction of the strange scholar were such that for the young Nuddea man to enter the lists with him at all was felt to be a piece of temerity. Thus parties were about equally divided —the old for Benares, the young for Nuddea— fairly ready to be swayed this way or that, as the contest might carry them. To us who read the tale, it is a foregone conclusion that Chaitanya was the abler disputant of the two. But we cannot forget that he was also the younger. Over and above this, he was at home. Under these circumstances we might have expected that some impulse of pity would tempt him to save the feeling of the older scholar. Nothing of the sort. The logical tournament has a chivalry of its own, but it is for truth, not for persons. Nothing must interfere with the effort to display the actual fact, and the assurance of this is closely bound up with the victory of one person or the other. So the debate proceeds remorselessly, without fear or favour, to its inevitable end in the triumph of youth and Nuddea. And we may be assured that nothing would have been so bitterly resented by the pundit from Benares as any idea that his age or his fame or his well-known achievements entitled him to be handled tenderly, as if with the gloves on.

But a system of high learning must have some points of contact with lay society. Especially is this the case when it is one of a nature that impoverishes its participants. There must be some means of gathering the sinews of war, in however scanty an amount. This need was met in India of the past by the fact that learning was looked upon as the brightest ornament of social life. No extraordinary marriage function in a great house could in those days be regarded as complete without its battle of the pundits. Invitations were sent out to members of rival schools to come and join their forces under the presidency and direction of such and such a Brahman. The contest would take place in the presence of the whole polite world, who, though they could not have waged it themselves, had quite sufficient knowledge of the language and matter under dispute to be keen and interested critics of skill. Put thus upon their mettle, the combatants would wrestle, and at the end of days or hours, as the case might be, the victor was declared. Sometimes the whole of the money-grant about to be made by the father of the bride would be assigned by him to the chief of the pundits. This would be for a signal and crushing victory. More often it would be a proportion of three-quarters, five-eighths, or even fifteen-sixteenths. Sometimes a man would indignantly refuse the award so graduated, feeling that it did not sufficiently recognise the fact that his rival had no ground left to stand upon. In this case a scholar of self-respect was willing to wait till he had driven the whole world to accept him on his own terms of all or nothing. As in the tournaments of European chivalry, the appearance of the unknown knight might at any moment occur, so here also one never knew whether some stranger of genius might not upset the best-calculated chances. The *savant* must be prepared to defend his own pre-eminence against all comers, and against every conceivable method, new or old.

But if this was the height of passion reached in such contests as took place in the presence of the comparatively learned, we can imagine what happened when scholars or *sadhus* themselves organised their own conferences amongst themselves. These were announced and financed by princes or by towns, and from far and wide, from remote unheard-of *tolls*, and from the libraries of palaces, as well as from great famous centres, arrived the scholars who were to take part. And when the struggle actually began,—ah! We have heard of the defeated taking a vow to starve himself to death, in his rage and mortification. We have heard of closely-fought sessions of many days at a stretch. And finally, when victory was declared, the conqueror, beside himself with the intoxication of success, would tear up the matting of the floor, in order to sprinkle dust, in token of contempt, upon the heads of grave and reverend adversaries.

In such occasions we have a glimpse of what may be called the post-graduate system of university-life. At places like Hrishikesh, we still have the remains of what have been great scholarly centres for the meeting of the monks and Brahmans. In the *Kumbh Mela,* which takes place at Hardwar, Allahabad, and Nasik by rotation, we have one of the most ancient and most learned assemblies of learning. The men who play their part here are not neophytes: they are already ripe scholars, meeting for mutual edification. Nor can we deny that there may be history in the tradition which says that at Hrishikesha, Vyasa collected and divided the four Vedas. Great works of scholarship might well be carried out by councils convened in some such way.

Thus we have a suggestion of the twofold development of Sanskritic education, one that of the school or college, the other that of the university proper. This last was more or less peripatetic, but none the less definite and real for that.

And the Brahmanic schools, on the other hand, were numerous and exact in their constitution. The student who arrived at twenty would sometimes stay in the *toll* till he was thirty-five, putting off the whole business of marriage and citizenship till his premier thirst for knowledge should be slaked. And yet were there "very few who arrived at Inference." In truth Inference like poetry was best left free. It was the crown and blossom of all a man had learnt. He had to study how to direct his argument with its "five limbs," which a modern world calls the major and minor premisses of the syllogism. He knew what fallacies to guard against, and how many modes of proof were possible. It was better for him that, being trained in all this, he should be left to steer his own course, alike in argument and belief, when it came to the application of his knowledge. It was better for men at large that opinions themselves should not be imparted or directed, although, if they rested on obvious fallacies, it would be well to expose them. Let him pursue wisdom, and with all his getting let him get understanding. Knowledge and wealth, in truth, were rival sisters, at the best. They appeared to be good friends, but there was between them a deep unspoken jealousy. Whoever paid honest court to the one would fail to win the unstinted largess of the other. On the other hand, each was compelled by the laws of courtesy to make a sufficient provision for her sister's worshipper. Thus the extremely rich man would not be an imbecile, nor the extremely learned left altogether to starve. There would be enough, but nothing over. Therefore let a man be clear from the first as to what he really wanted. Above all, let him never pursue after knowledge as a means to wealth. Gifts in the old days were largely made in kind. Hence there came into the *toll* enough rice to feed the students from year to year, and yet the whole treasure of the *guru's* wife would be a few silver ornaments and a supply of brass cooking-vessels! Truly the highest labour for humanity is never paid. Indeed, unless the enthusiasm of his women-folk was as great as his own, it is difficult to see how the guru could ever have kept a *toll* at all. For the wife had to see to the cooking, and cleaning, and the nursing of the sick. Every disciple looked upon her as his mother, and the bond of reverence and affection was as real as that which bound him to his master himself. In the case of her being widowed, the disciples were responsible for her maintenance and protection. They must beg for her if need be. The relation was really one of a mother and her sons. Of this parental tie that bound the pupil to his master and his master's household we catch numerous glimpses in the poems and history of the Indian people. One of the first episodes in the Mahabharata is the story of Devajani, whose love gathered round the strange youth Kacha, the student-brother, who had come to her father to learn his mystic lore. He has come in truth from the land of the gods, to master the learning of men. And very solemnly and beautifully is that wisdom consecrated, as he gathers it, by being first put to the test for the aid and deliverance of his master himself. When five years are over, and Kacha must return to his own land, Devajani cannot believe that they are to be parted, and begs to be taken with him as his wife. But the disciple of her father regards her as his sister, and the idea is impossible to him. It is then that the beautiful Devajani curses him in her despair with the future sterility of the knowledge he has acquired. He accepts the curse in so far as it concerns himself, yet adds with a note of triumph, "But in him it shall bear fruit to whom I shall impart it!"

The great Akbar, in something of the same spirit, it is said, at a later date made attempts to win from the Brahmans of Benares a knowledge of the Vedic scales and cadences, but always without success. At last he determined on a fraud. One morning, shortly after, as one of the chief Brahmans went to bathe, he found on the *ghât* a Brahman youth fainting with hunger, who said he had come far to learn from him the Vedas. The compassionate pundit took the lad home, and kept him as a disciple and son, and in course of time he fell in love with the daughter of his master and asked for her hand in marriage. The scholar loved the youth, who was of a most noble and promising disposition, and at the end of the training his request was to be granted. But the young man could not bring himself to carry his deception so far, and on the eve of his wedding-day he revealed the fact that he was a Mohammedan. The Brahman did not withdraw his promise or his blessing. But he saw that the sacred trust of his art was broken, the purity of his line was to be lost for ever. And he insisted, it is said, upon dying by fire, as a penance for the twofold betrayal that he had unwittingly committed.

In the culture that characterised India then before the dawn of English education, we have seen that the severer forms of learning were an occasion of criticism and delight to non-Brahmanical society, even as high musical skill is appreciated in Europe by all classes. But the finer flowers of literary culture were left to be absorbed and augmented spontaneously. Philosophy, logic, and even the chanting of ancient texts might be corrected and regulated, but creativeness was accepted as the grace of God, the only safeguard put upon it being that, as the man trained in reasoning could not be misled by false argument, so the man trained in any fine and arduous form of mental activity could not admire what was wanting in nobility and beauty.

So elaborate an organisation argues authorities of some kind at its birth. We see here a university system which must have been nursed and protected by powerful influence for many centuries. In this connection we cannot but remember that the glory of the great Gupta throne of Pataliputra, in the fourth and fifth centuries, was inextricably bound up, as that house deeply realised, with the fate of Sanskrit learning and literature. Those were days in which the decline of the Buddhist orders had not yet begun. For the moment, the great university of Nalanda was at the zenith of its power. It carried on its researches in a dozen branches of knowledge in Sanskrit. It was the state observatory, and constituted the official meridian ; for there, and there alone, we are told by Hiouen Tsang, was kept the state water-clock, which regulated time for the whole of Magadha. Its fame attracted students not only from all parts of India, but from the empire of China itself. It is told of Nalanda, in the family histories of Vikrampur, that it had five hundred professors, and that on one occasion at least the head of them all was a man from the village of Vajra Yogini in Vikrampur—so far back stretched the memory of the glory of scholars in an Indian pedigree.

Our last clear glimpse of Nalanda is in the middle of the seventh century at the visit of Hiouen Tsang. At the beginning of the ninth century again the curtain rises on the life and career of Sankaracharya. The stories told of the arguments and discussions by which he ousted Buddhist monks grown ignorant and illiterate, from the charge of sacred places, and handed them over to his own men, show that the system of Sanskritic culture was already more or less complete. We cannot help believing that the organisation of Brahmanical learning must have been a reflection of a still earlier organisation of Buddhistic learning, that the life lived till the other day in a Bengali *toll* must be an exact replica of the life lived in an earlier period in such places as the caves of Ajanta or Ellora. But in this system of scholarly contest, to the verdict of which the Buddhists themselves submitted so far as in defeat to render up the care of their sacred places to their conquerors, we seem to catch a glimpse of something older still, something dating from the primæval world itself.

The assemblies of the *sadhus* and their public discussions of the debatable points, constituted an organisation already perfect perhaps in the Gupta period, and in the very prime of its influence and activity in the era of Sankaracharya. In Bengal the empire of Gour was to last undisturbed another four centuries, and to succumb in its entirety only to the genius of Shere Shah and the later Moghuls. This empire of Gour deliberately linked with itself the ecclesiastical *shava* of the Kanauji Brahmans, who remained beside the throne as a kind of pontifical court, nursing institutions and deciding interpretations as long as the dynasty lasted. We cannot refuse to see in this strong and prolonged national independence the real reason for the high degree of elaboration attained by Sanskritic culture in Bengal. A geographical *cul-de-sac* is always the place to look for the integrity of customs and institutions elsewhere disintegrated by foreign conquest. According to this law, we might expect to find in the southern apex of Dekkan, and in Eastern Bengal, traces of the past still vigorous, when in other parts they had disappeared. In the lingering memory of the life of the *tolls* and the learned combats of the wedding parties we have such a remnant of the mediæval world, and it speaks with no uncertain sound. Mithila, Nuddea, and Vikrampur were sparks from fire that had been Nalanda. Benares, Hrishikesh, Nasik, and Ujjain still remain to testify to us of a time when the life of mind and spirit ranked above temporal good in the minds of the forefathers. They were parts of an immense conflagration of learning, which it should be the business of India's sons once more to set alight.

THE CITY IN CLASSICAL EUROPE: A VISIT TO POMPEII

IT is in the cities of classical Europe that we might expect to find the most perfect and unconfused expression of the civic sense. For *religion* meant to the Roman neither more nor less than the sum-total of those institutions and ideas which serve as a binding-force to unite together, *to tie together*, groups of men. Thus nothing was so vital to him, nothing was in so real a sense his *dharma*, his essential ideal, as his conception of the city-state. Compared with him, even the Greek was Asiatic and theocratic. The Acropolis or the mausoleum, the university, the temple, or the tomb, far out-topped in his case the sanctity of court and market-place, of home and commune. But to the Roman, on the contrary, the open Forum—built in a fashion not unlike that of an elongated mosque—where citizens assembled to discuss public affairs, to hold meetings, and to celebrate festivals, the open Forum was at once the heart, brain, and lungs of the civic organism. Here men entered as citizens; here they heard the public news; here they made their political opinions felt. The Forum was at once an informal senate and a club, and it was the one essential feature that made the sum-total of a group of buildings surrounded by walls into that something more which we name a city.

Clearly however if we want to study the classical city in detail, the ideal means of doing so would be to discover one which had been arrested at that particular stage in its development. Rome herself has become since then a city of priests and churches. She is the cradle of Christianity, not classical at all. Marseilles was never more than colonial, and is now post-mediæval and modern. By a strange catastrophe however which we dare not call good fortune even for archæologists, a catastrophe that happened one summer day more than eighteen hundred years ago, one such city has been preserved for us under precisely these ideal conditions. It is now more than a hundred and fifty years since the long sleep of Pompeii under the ashes of Vesuvius was disturbed. From the 23rd of August in the year A.D. 79 till 1748, the peasant ploughed and reaped, gardens blossomed and orchards flourished, in the soil above the ancient streets, and none knew or dreamed of the awful drama that had once been enacted beneath their feet. To-day, most of Pompeii stands uncovered within its walls, and if one enters by the ancient *Porta della Marina*, the gate towards the sea, and goes into the little museum on the right, one finds record enough, the more vivid in that it is unwritten, of that hour of sudden death. There are students who are said to decipher the whole story of a human soul from a specimen of a handwriting. There are others who do the same by the palm of the hand or the sole of the foot. But here in the museum at Pompeii we find a surer means of divination than any of these. In the solid mass of fine ashes which fell over the doomed city on that awful 23rd of August, numbers of people were buried in the act of flight. And in recent excavations it has been found possible to make casts of several of their bodies, by filling the form in which they had lain with plaster of Paris. The bodies themselves, it must be understood, have been carbonised and long ago disappeared, but a kind of shell was formed round each of them, under the pressure of the hot ashes, and into this hollow shell plaster could be poured so as to take the exact place of the corpse that once lay there. This is the origin of the figures which lie in the cases down the length of the museum. The forms are naked, for the reason that the clothing must have caked in the ashes and formed part of the mass about them.

Never were seen symbols at once so graphic and so tragic. It is the very act of death we see before us. The human mind has smitten its own indelible record of one brief moment on the only writing surface that is absolutely within its power, the prisoning body. Oh what sentences are these! They reveal the past of the soul, as well as the dread moment of inscription. Here is a man, who has fallen backwards with his hands thrown up;

on the breathless lips we hear the gasp of despair, and from the sightless eyes see flashed back the last picture they saw, the horror of the blast of fire that met him from before, even as he found his knees buried in the rising dust below. Here again is a woman unaccustomed to struggle. She has fallen forward, and her head is pillowed on her arm. Like the man, it was death she met in her hurried flight. But she met it with something like resignation. Her whole attitude speaks of submission, of sweetness, of grace. Surely at the last there was a touch of peace. It may be that she was the last of her household, that the safety of her children was assured. It may be she was comforting some other, showing someone about her how to die. Indian women also have met deaths as terrible with this gentle acceptance, or even with exultant triumph.

But we leave these graphs of the spirit stamped upon the human body, and proceed to examine that other record, the city itself, built by generation upon generation of men, through nigh upon a thousand years. In form it was of a type familiar enough to us in India. Conjeeveram to this day, or even the Hindu quarter of Calcutta, can furnish us with something very like it.

The Street of Abundance and the Street of Fortune were indeed, as their names imply, full of rich men's houses. But they were narrow, as is natural in sunny climates, where light is desired to fall subdued between the houses. They were so narrow that two chariots could not pass, as the deep ruts for a single pair of wheels bear evidence. But they had footpaths, and perpetual stepping-stones across the roadways from one to the other tell tales of the heavy summer rains. They show us another thing also: that probably the chariots were driven in every case by a pair of horses. There was no entanglement of traffic, however, such as is known to us, for people did not drive hither and thither in the city, but only in or out of it, and the ways to other places were definitely laid down and mapped—the gate to the sea, the gate to Herculaneum, and so on, and vehicles went always in a single known direction. In the Street of Mercury we have a couple of memorials which tell us much, arches built in commemoration of visits paid to the town by Caligula and Nero. They tell us in the first place of a couple of days of civic festival. The same arches would be made by ourselves with bamboo wands and flags and flowers, and pulled down in a day or two, and the occasion forgotten. They were in these cases made of stone, intended to be eternal. And truly, two thousand years later, they will still be able to revive the uproarious scenes of those two days of pleasure! But they tell us still more. They reveal to us the whole character of the city. It was a week-end place, a city of pleasure, a garden-city—not using that term in the decorous modorn sense! Caligula and Nero were the most profligate of Roman Emperors, and doubtless, in coming to Pompeii and being received there with enthusiasm, they came unto their own. We can imagine that ancient tales of Sodom and Gomorrah, destroyed in fire by reason of their wickedness, were not without their application to the case of Pompeii. And yet the beauty of the situation, of the culture of the inhabitants would always offer the possibility of a lofty enjoyment also; and Cicero, we are told, retired to his house there to write.

It does not need the Street of Tombs—where the so-called graves are only monuments covering repositories for cinerary urns—to remind us of the similarity between the civilisation of Rome and that of high-caste Hinduism. The houses themselves consist of rooms built round an outer and inner courtyard. In the most perfect of all that have yet been discovered, the home of the Vetii, the inner courtyard, and the kitchen with its clay-built stove and metal *dekhchis*, are eloquent of this similarity. In the middle of the outer court is found in every case a small marble tank, built doubtless for ablutions of face and hands or feet. In the inner court of the Vetii, which may have offered hospitality—who knows?—to emperors on their visits to Pompeii, there is a multiplicity of small raised basin fountains, probably used for this purpose as well as for ornament. For actual bathing, we have a fresco of the bath of Diana, which shows that a vase of water to be poured over the person was as much the method of the Pompeian as of the Hindu. And there were also the magnificent public baths, of which those of the Forum must have constituted the most fashionable club-house of the city. Especially was this true of the tepidarium, or middle hall, where bathers who had already put off the outer garments could sit or stand for warmth about a large bronze brazier which acted as a hearth, while they prepared themselves for the bath by using the oils and essences taken from the niches in the walls. In the streets outside are laid bare the metal pipes, stamped in relief with the names of the makers, by which water was conveyed to houses and baths from the town-reservoirs. But in the streets too we find water-troughs with raised drinking-fountains, offering refreshments to man and beast. And in one case the stone edge is worn where the hands of generations of drinkers have rested, as they leaned over it to fill their cups at the tap and drink. Ah! the pathos of such silent witness to the busy life that once filled the empty world about us. Here in the market-hall, when it was first excavated, was found a little heap of fish-bones, where the stall of fried fish had been, and where already a number of people had eaten on that last dread day, before its tragic noon. The ruts worn deep in the paved roads by the wheels of carts and chariots; the snake approaching a nest of eggs, that we see so constantly painted on the walls as a warning to passers-by that these streets are sacred to Æsculapius, the God of hygiene and cleanliness; the notice, again, painted on the walls in red letters, as the equivalent of the modern poster; it is by such trifles as these that the deepest emotion of Pompeii is conveyed. Life, common, everyday, vivacious, duly compounded of the trivial and the great, brought suddenly to a stop—this is the spectacle that we have before us, the spectacle of one bright summer morning unexpectedly made eternal by death.

There were shops in these streets scattered up and down amongst the residences. And it is interesting to think for a moment of the kinds that could not be preserved. Obviously stores of cloth would be destroyed. Nor can we imagine the steps of the public buildings without their country-people bearing baskets of fruit and flowers and vegetables from without the city. Of these, however, there necessarily remains no trace. But the bakers' shops are there, with their ovens and their millstones; even, in one case, with their loaves in the closed oven, carbonised but intact. And the oil-shops remain, though the oil is long ago dried into the empty vessels. And the wine-shops abound. Truly was Pompeii a city of temptations!

It is in the Basilica and the Forum, however, that one arrives at the classical significance of Pompeii. There was an older forum, small and triangular in shape, containing a significant little Temple of the Thunderbolt, and the fall of a meteor may well have been the original reason for building the city on the chosen spot. But at the time of its historic catastrophe the town had much increased, and had built for itself a new and larger forum. A long open space in the middle is surrounded on three sides by a columned pavement, and at the far end, facing the ring of deep-blue mountains in the background which forms the glory of the site, a temple of Jupiter stands on a tremendously high platform, the altar of public sacrifice. Here we can see the citizens pacing up and down, or meeting in earnest groups to discuss or gossip. Here we can see the couriers come in with public news from Rome. Here in the middle the orators addressed the crowds. Or here, again, the citizens thronged, whatever their personal creed or habits, to watch, on appointed days of public festival, the slaying of the sacrificial bull. Immediately adjoining is the Basilica or High Court. Again we have the same plan of buildings, but the aisles here were probably roofed, and the nave alone left open. And here, to judge from the magnificence of the appointments, it would appear that the legal and judicial aspects of life absorbed as large a share of the intellect of Roman as of modern civilisation. At the end may be seen the great statues and the sacred symbol of justice which screened from public view the high cell or apartment in which the judge listened to opposite pleadings and sentenced the accused. In the cell below this däised chamber the prisoners awaited their turns, while the door at the bottom of the short staircase was guarded doubtless by a couple of men-at-arms. Outside, the aisles of the Basilica formed a kind of cloister—or Bar Library—in which the rival lawyers met, walked, and talked.

In its religious aspects the life of Pompeii was confused enough. Here is the temple of an Egyptian deity, here again of a Greek. The two-faced image of Janus, native to the soil, is confronted by the new-fangled worship of the Emperor. Who knows but the hope spoken in Christianity had been whispered behind some of these roofless walls, ere there arrived the hour of their destruction? Religion appears to be largely, with these Romans, an act of reverence to the ancestors, a wise pact with the powerful Infinite to guard the home. But when we come to their public buildings, and to the organisation of their public life, to their theatres and their fencing-schools, their monuments and their statues, their court of justice and their forum, we have reached a stronghold which they hold with no uncertain grasp. In civic organisation, in the civic consciousness they are supreme, these doughty Romans; and when they become a circle of predatory peoples, theocratic countries, alarmed for their own survival, may learn at their feet of that efficient self-organisation which is the beginning of strength. Wherever the seed of India has been blown, it has grown up into world-faiths: wherever the seed of Rome has fallen, it has raised up mighty nations. Its action may lie in terror; its reaction produces strength.

A STUDY OF BENARES

EVEN in great places we cannot always command the passive moments of rare insight. It was already my third visit to Benares when I sat one day, at an hour after noon, in the Vishwanath Bazar. Everything about me was hushed and drowsy. The *sadhu*-like shopkeepers nodded and dozed over their small wares; here the weaving of girdle or scapulary with a *mantram*, there a collection of small stone Shivas. There was little enough of traffic along the narrow footway, but overhead went the swallows by the invisible roadways of the blue, flying in and out among their nests in the eaves. And the air was filled with their twittering, and with the sighing resonance of the great bell in the Temple of Vishweswar, as the constant stream of barefooted worshippers entered, and prayed, and before departing touched it. Swaying, sobbing, there it hung, seeming as if in that hour of peace it were some mystic dome, thrilled and responsive to every throb of the city's life. One could believe that these ripples of sound that ran across it were born of no mechanical vibration, but echoed, here a moan, there a prayer, and yet again a cry of gladness, in all the distant quarters of Benares:

R

that the bell was even as a great weaver, weaving into unity of music, and throwing back on earth, those broken and tangled threads of joy and pain that without it would have seemed so meaningless and so confused.

A step beyond were the shops of the flower-sellers, who sell white flowers for the worship of Shiva across the threshold. Oh what a task, to spend the whole of life, day after day, in this service only, the giving of the flowers for the image of the Lord! Has there been no soul that, occupied thus, has dreamed and dreamed itself into *Mukti*, through the daily offering?

And so came to me the thought of the old minsters of Europe, and of what it meant to live thus, like the swallows and the townsfolk and the flowers, ever in the shadow of a great cathedral. For that is what Benares is—a city built about the walls of a cathedral.

It is common to say of Benares that it is curiously modern, and there is on the face of it a certain truth in the statement. For the palaces and monasteries and temples that line the banks of the Ganges between the mouths of Barna and Asi have been built for the most part within the last three hundred years. There is skill and taste enough in India yet to rebuild them all again, if they fell to-morrow. Benares as she stands is in this sense the work of the Indian people as they are to-day.

But never did any city so sing the song of the

Photo: Johnston and Hoffmann

BENARES

past. One is always catching a hint of reminiscence in the bazars, in the interior, and in the domestic architecture. Here is the Jammu *Chhattra* for instance, built in the Jaunpur Pathan style, common in Northern India from the twelfth to the fourteenth centuries. Not far off again, we have a glimpse of a roof-balustrade that retains many of the characteristics of an Asokan rail, so clearly is it a wooden fence rendered in stone. I have seen a pillared hall too, in a house looking out upon the Ganges, that might almost have known the two thousand years that its owners claimed for it. And here in the bazar of Vishwanath we are treading still, it may be, that very pathway through the forest that was followed by the Vedic forefathers, when first they saw the sun rise on the East of the great river, and offered the *Hom* where the golden grate of Vishweswar stands to-day, chanting their *rijks* in celebration of worship.[1]

Nothing holds its place longer than a road. The winding alleys between the backs of houses and gardens in European cities may, at no distant date, have been paths through meadows and cornfields. And similarly, in all countries, a footway is apt to be a silent record of unwritten history. But who shall recover the story of this little street, or write the long long poem of the lives and deaths of those whose feet have passed to and forth along its flagstones in four thousand years?

[1] The allusion here is not only to the Sanskrit *rijk*, but also to the early Norse *rijks* and *runes*.

Truly the city, even as she stands, is more ancient than any superficial critic would suppose. It was here at Sarnath, in the year 583 B.C. or thereabouts, that the great message pealed out whose echoes have never died away in history, "Open ye your ears, O Monks, the deliverance from death is found!" And the importance which the Deer-Park thus assumes in the life of Buddha, both before and after the attainment of Nirvana, sufficiently proves its importance as the university of philosophy of its own age. Three hundred years later Asoka, seeking to build memorials of all the most sacred events in the history of his great Master, was able, as the recent excavations show us, to make a tiny stupa with its rail in some cell, by that time already underground, whose site had been especially sanctified by the touch of Buddha's feet. We thus learn, not only that the Deer-Park of Benares (so called, probably, because pains were taken to keep it cleared of larger game) was important in the year 583 B.C. and again in 250 B.C., but also that it was sufficiently a centre of resort throughout the intervening period to guarantee its maintenance of an unbroken tradition with regard to points of extremely minute detail. But it was not Sarnath alone that saw the coming and going of Buddha in the birth of the great enlightenment. Nor was it the Abkariyeh Kand alone that had already formed an important religious centre for ages before the early Mohammedan period. The very name of the Dasasvamedh Ghât and Bazar commemorates a period long enough to have included ten imperial sacrifices, each one of which must have represented at least a reign. Probably throughout the Pataliputra age, that is to say from 350 B.C. to A.D. 528, Benares was the ecclesiastical and sacrificial seat of empire. It contains at least two Asokan pillars, one in the grounds of the Queen's College, and the other, as we now know, at the entrance to the old-time Monastery of Sarnath. And we know with certainty that in the youth of Buddha it was already a thriving industrial centre. For the robes that he threw aside, perhaps in the year 590 B.C., to adopt the *gerua* of the *sannyasin*, are said in many books to have been made of Benares silk.

But this is in truth only what we might have expected. For the water-way is always in early ages the chief geographical feature of a country, and the position of Benares at the northward bend of the river determines the point of convergence for all the foot-roads of the South and East, and makes her necessarily the greatest distributing centre in India. Thus she constitutes a palimpsest, not a simple manuscript, of cities. One has here been built upon another; period has accumulated upon period. There are houses in the crowded quarters whose foundations are laid, as it were, in mines of bricks, and whose owners live upon the sale of these ancestral wares. And there is at least one temple that I know of whose floor is eight or ten feet below the level of the present street, and whose date is palpably of the second to the fourth century after Christ.

If then we may compare large things with small, Benares may be called the Canterbury of the Asokan and post-Asokan India. What Delhi became later to the militarised India of the Rajput and the Moslem, that Benares had already been to an earlier India, whose eastern provinces had seen Buddha. At Sarnath the memory of the great *Sannyasin* was preserved by the devoted members of a religious order, either Buddhist or Jain. At Benares the Brahmans laboured, as citizens and householders, to enforce the lesson that none of his greatness was lacking in the Great God. The Shiva, clad in the tigerskin and seated in meditation like a Buddha, who is carved in low relief at the entrance to Elephanta in the harbour of Bombay, was the Hindu ideal of the later Buddhist period. And so the Vedic city, through whose streets had passed the Blessed One, became the sacred city of Shiva; and to make and set up his emblem there—the form in stone of the formless God—was held for long ages after the same act of merit that the erecting of votive stupas had so long been in places of Buddhistic pilgrimage. Nay, even now old stupas remain of the early Puranic period, and early Shivas of a later phase of development, about the streets and *ghâts* of Benares, to tell of the impress made by Buddha on an age that was then already passing away.

But Benares is not only an Indian Canterbury,

it is also an Oxford. Under the shadow of temples and monasteries cluster the schools and dwellings of the pundits or learned Sanskritists, and from all parts of India the poor students flock there to study the classics and ancient rituals of Hinduism. The fame of Nuddea is in her Sanskrit logic, but that of Benares in her philosophy and Brahman lore. Thus she remains ever the central authority on questions of worship and of the faith, and her influence is carried to all ends of India by every wandering scholar returning to his own province. It is a mediæval type of culture, of course, carried out in the mediæval way. It takes a man twelve years here to exhaust a single book, while under the modern comparative method we are compelled to skim the surfaces of a score or more in a single year. It follows that we have here a study of the contents rather than the relations of a given work; significance rather than co-ordination. But for this very reason the Benares-trained scholar is of his own kind, secure in his type, as fearless in his utterance of that which he knows as those other mediævalists in a modern world, John Bunyan and William Blake.

But in Benares as a culture-centre even in the present generation, though it is fast vanishing, we have another extraordinary advantage to note. Being as she is the authoritative seat of Hinduism and Sanskrit learning, the city stands nevertheless, side by side with Jaunpur, the equally authoritative centre of Mussulmân learning in India. She represents in fact the dividing line between the Sanskritic civilisation of the Hindu provinces and the Persian and Arabic culture of the Mohammedan. And consequently she still has members of a class that once constituted one of the most perfect types of national education in the world, elderly Hindu gentlemen who were trained in their youth not only to read Sanskrit literature, but also to read and enjoy what was then the distinctive accomplishment of royal courts, namely Persian poetry. And the mind that is born of this particular synthesis—rendered possible in Benares by the presence on the one hand of the Hindu pundit and the neighbourhood on the other of the Jaunpur *maulvi*—is not that of a great scholar certainly, but it is that of a member of the wide world, polished, courtly, and urbane. One of the most charming forms of high breeding that humanity has known will be lost with the last well-born Hindu who has had the old time training in Persian. Nor indeed can anyone who has seen modern and mediæval culture side by side, as we may still sometimes see them in Asia, doubt that the true sense of literature is the prerogative of the mediævalist.

Benares, then, is an informal university. And like other universities of the Middle Ages, it has always supported its scholars and students by a vast network of institutions of mutual aid. It is no disgrace there for a boy to beg his bread, when love of learning has brought him a thousand miles on foot. Nor was it in mediæval Leipzig, or

Heidelberg, or Oxford. These are the scholars for whom our schools and colleges were founded. The wives of the burghers expected to contribute to the maintenance of such. And it is in Benares only food that is wanted. In the dark hours of one winter morning, as I made my way through the Bengalitollah to the bathing-*ghâts*, I could hear in the distance the sound of Sanskrit chanting. And soon I came up to a student who had slept all night on the stone verandah of some well-to-do house, screened from the bitterest pinch of cold by carefully-drawn walls of common sacking, and now had risen before five to read by the light of a hurricane lamp and commit to memory his task for the day. Further on another studied, with no such luxuries as canvas walls and paraffin lamp. He had slept all night under his single blanket on the open stone, and the tiny Indian *batti* was the light by which he was reading now.

Here is love of learning with labour and poverty. It is obviously impossible for these to earn their bread in addition to performing the tasks imposed by their schools. The spontaneous benefactions of rich nobles and merchants were doubtless enough in the Middle Ages—when religious enthusiasm was high, and the problem still limited—to maintain the pundits in whose houses the students lived. But in modern times the institution of the *chhattras* has grown up, and it is said that in the city there are three hundred and sixty-five of these. A *chhattra* is a house at which a given number of persons receive a meal daily. Some give double doles. Some give to others besides Brahmans. Many have been themselves the gifts of pious widows, and a few of kings. But that it is the duty of the city to provide food for her scholars all are agreed. Is not Benares to these children of Shiva Annapurna the Mother, She whose hand is ever "full of grain"?

But Benares is more than the precincts of a group of temples. She is more even than a university, and more than the historic and industrial centre of three thousand years. The solemn Manikarnika stands rightly in the centre of her river-front. For she is a great national *shmashan,* a vast burning-*ghât.* "He who dies in Benares attains Nirvana." The words may be nothing but an expression of intense affection. Who would not love to die on those beautiful *ghâts,* with the breath of the night or the morning on his brow, the sound of temple-bells and chanting in his ears, and the promises of Shiva and memories of the past in his heart? Such a death, embraced in an ecstasy, would it not in itself be *Mukti,* the goal? "Oh Thou great *Jnanam,* that art God, dwell thou in me!" Such was the vision that broke upon one who bent from the flower-seller's balcony to see evensong chanted by the Brahmans round the blossom-crowned Vishweswar. And never again can that mind think of God as seated on a throne, with His children kneeling round Him, for to it the secret has been shown that Shiva is within the heart of man, and He is the Absolute Consciousness, the Infinite Knowledge, and the Unconditioned Bliss. Which of us would not die, if we could, in the place that was capable of flashing such a message across the soul?

All India feels this. All India hears the call. And one by one, step by step, with bent head and bare feet for the most part, come those, chiefly widows and *sadhus*, whose lives are turned away from all desire save that of a holy death. How many monuments of *sati* are to be seen in Benares, one on the Manikarnika Ghât, and many dotted about the fields and roads outside! These are the memorials of triumphant wifehood in the hour of its bereavement. But there are other triumphs. Clothed and veiled in purest white, bathing, fasting, and praying continually, here in the hidden streets of Benares dwell thousands of those whose lives are one long effort to accumulate merit for the beloved second self. And if the scholar be indeed the servant of the nation, is the saint less? The lamp of ideal womanhood, burning in the sheltered spot at the feet of the image, and "not flickering," is this, or is it not, as a light given to the world?

Benares, again, is an epitome of the whole Indian synthesis of nationality. As the new-comer is rowed down the river past the long lines of temples and bathing-*ghâts*, while the history of each is told to him in turn, he feels, catching his breath at each fresh revelation of builded beauty, that all roads in India always must have led to Benares. Here is the monastery of Kedarnath, the headquarters of the southern monks, which represents to the province of Madras all the merits of Himalayan pilgrimage. Here again is the *ghât* of Ahalya Bai Rani, the wonderful widowed Mahratta Queen, whose temples and roads and tanks remain all over India to witness to the greatness of the mother heart in rulers. Or behind this we may see the *Math* of Sankaracharya's order, the high caste *Dandis*, whose line is unbroken and orthodoxy unimpeached from the days of their founder, early in the ninth century, till the present hour. Again, we see the palace of the Nagpore Bhonslas (now in the hands of the Maharaja of Darbhanga), connecting Benares with the memory of the Mahratta power, and further on the royal buildings of Gwalior and even of Nepal. Nor is everything here dedicated to Shiva, Shiva's city though it be. For here again we come on the temple of *Beni Madhab*, one of the favourite names of Vishnu. Even Mohammedan sovereigns could not submit to be left out. Secular science is embodied in the beautiful old Mân Mandir of Akbar's time, with its instruments and lecture-hall, and the Mussulmân faith in the towering minarets of Aurungzeb's mosque.

But what is true of the Ganges front becomes still more clear when we pass behind and consider the city as a whole. Ranjit Singh made no separate building, but he linked Vishweswar irrevocably

Photo: Johnston and Hoffmann

THE GHÁTS, BENARES

with Amritsar, when he covered its roof with gold. Zemindars of Bengal, Sirdars of the Punjab, and nobles of Rajputana, all have vied with one another in leaving temples and shrines, charities and benefactions, dotted over the *Panch Kos*.

Or we may see the same thing industrially. We can buy in Benares, besides her own delicate webs, the *saris* of Madras and the Dekkan alike. Or we may go to the Vishwanath Bazar for the carpentry of the Punjab. We may find in the same city the brass work of Nasik, of Trichinopoli, and of the Nepalese frontier. It is there, better than anywhere else in India, that we may buy the stone vessels of Gaya, of Jubbulpur, and of Agra, or the Shivas of the Nerbudda and the *salagrams* of the Gumti and Nepal. And the food of every province may be bought in these streets, the language of every race in India heard within these walls.

On questions of religion and of custom, again, in all parts of India, as has been said, the supreme appeal is to Benares. The princes of Gwalior dine only when the news has been telegraphed that the day's food has been offered here. Here too the old works of art and religion, and the old craftsmen practising quaint crafts, linger longest, and may still perchance be found when they have become rare to the point of vanishing everywhere else. Here the *Vyasas* chant authoritative renderings of the epic stories on the *ghâts*. And here, at great banquets food is still considered only secondary to the reciting of the scriptures. Surely it is clear enough that as in the Latin Empire of City and of Church the saying grew up, "All roads lead to Rome," so also in India, so long as she remains India, all roads, all faiths, all periods, and all historical developments will lead us sooner or later back to Benares.

A city in such a position, possessed of such manifold significance, the pilgrim-centre of a continent, must always have had an overwhelming need of strong civic organisation. And that such a need was recognised in the city during the ages of its growth, we may see in many ways. No mediæval township in Europe gives stronger evidence of self-organisation than we find here.

"The mediæval city," says the great European sociologist Kropotkin, "appears as a double federation: of all householders united into small territorial unions—the street, the parish, the section—and of individuals united by oath into guilds, according to their professions; the former being a product of the village-community origin of the city, while the second is a subsequent growth, called into life by new conditions."

This is a master statement which can at once be applied here, if only we dismiss the European idea of labour as the main *motif* of this city's growth, and substitute the Indian equivalent of religion and learning. Labour is present here of course, and has flourished, as we know, in this spot, during at least three thousand years, but it has never reared its head to become a predominant and independent factor in the growth of Benares. This central significance, this higher element in the federation, has been supplied here, by the presence of priests and pundits, monasteries and poets, bound to each other, not by professional oaths, but by the invisible and spiritual bonds of caste and tradition, and religious bonds—by Hinduism, in short. Not the craftsman, but the Hindu carrying the craftsman with him, has made Benares what she is, and here in this city we have the picture of one of the finest things that the Indian faith—uninterfered with by foreign influences, and commanding the enthusiastic co-operation of the whole nation—could produce. It is no mean achievement. On Benares as it has made it the Hindu genius may well take its stand. By the city of Shiva it may well claim to be judged.

It is, however, when we turn to the first element in Kropotkin's analysis of the city that we find Benares to be most completely illuminated. In a pilgrim-city, we cannot but think that some mutual organisation of householders for self-defence must have been a prime necessity. The policing of such a city was more than usually important. What were the arrangements made for sanitation, for ambulance, for hospital-service, for the clearing-out of vagrants? These things may not in the Middle Ages have been called by these names, but assuredly their realities existed, and such necessities had to be met. Householders united into small territorial unions—the street, the *para*. And is not

Benares filled with small courts and alleys, divided from the main streets by short flights of broad steps, each crowned by its own gate? Is it more than thirty or forty years since each of these had its own guard or *concierge* and was closed at night to be opened again in the morning? In many cases of course the massive doors themselves are now removed, but the pillars and hooks and hinges still remain to bear witness to their old function. In other instances they stand there still pushed back against the wall, and one pauses a moment as one passes to ask, When was this last shut? These portals to each little group of important houses are a silent witness to the order and cleanliness of Benares as the Hindu made it. Just as in Edinburgh, as in Nürnberg, as in Paris, so here also, the group of wealthy houses thus barred in at a certain hour after dark was responsible for the freedom of its own space from uncleanliness and violence. It must undertake the connection between its own sanitation and the underground sewage system of the city, which was similar in character to that of ancient Pataliputra. It must be responsible for the proper alleviation of such suffering as fell within its limits, and its members must duly contribute their full share to the common burdens of the city as a whole. But when we come to the gates of the *para* or section, of which some still remain guarded by their watchmen outstanding in the bazaars, we understand the full importance to the mediæval mind of the question of civic order and of a strong but peaceful civic defence. For here within these gateways, we find the shrines of *Kal Bhairab*, the divine *Kotwal*, who perambulates the city of Shiva night after night, with staff and dog, who is worshipped by sentinels and gate-keepers, and who has the supreme discretion of accepting or rejecting at his will those who fain would enter within the sacred bounds. Of the divine *Kotwal* every city-watchman held himself as minister and earthly representative. And in this worship of *Kal Bhairab*, the Black Demon of Shiva, we may read the whole history of the civic organisation of Benares in the Middle Ages.

The modern age was later perhaps in arriving, here than elsewhere. But arrive it did, and its work when it came, here as elsewhere, was to multiply problems and to discredit the solutions that had been discovered by slow ages of growth. All that strong rope of self-defence, twisted of so many strands of local combination and territorial responsibility, with which Benares had been wont to meet her own needs, was now done away. The communal sense was stunned by the blow, for the fact was demonstrated to it *ad nauseam* that it was itself powerless against strong central combinations of force. Thus the old self-jurisdiction and self-administration of the civic group was banished. And at the same time the railways connected Benares with every part of India, and made it possible to pour in upon her daily as large a number of diseased, infirm, and starving persons, as may once have reached her on foot or in boats in the course of a year. Thus a forest of needs has grown up in modern Benares, of which the past generations with their common-sense, their spontaneous kindliness, and their thrifty municipal management, knew nothing.

Poor working-folk come, when the last hope has failed them, trusting that the Great God will be their refuge in his own city. In the old days, when Benares was a wealthy capital, these would have made their way to some house or *para* inhabited by well-to-do townsfolk from their own district, and through their kind offices work would sooner or later have been found. But now they find themselves amongst strangers. The music of temple-bells is the only sound familiar to them. Priests and fellow-worshippers are alike unknown. And it may be that in the sanctuary-city they have but fled from one despair to another.

Or the poor student comes here to learn. In the old days he would have found house-room as well as food in the home of his guru, or of some wealthy patron, and if he fell ill, he would have been cared for there, as a member of the family. To-day the number of so-called students is great, and possibly amongst them the indolent are many. For certainly temptations must have multiplied, at the same time that the moral continuity of the old relation between distant homestead and metropolitan *para* has been lost. In any case, even amongst the most earnest, some of these poor students have,

WORSHIP.

From Water-colour by Nanda Lal Bose.

as we have seen, to live in the streets. And when illness overtakes such there is none to aid, for there is none even to know. The *chhattras* are certainly a wonderful institution, showing the unexpected power of this ancient city to meet the needs of her own children. But the *chhattras* cannot offer home and hospital. And these also are sometimes needed.

And finally there is the case of the widowed gentlewomen who come to Benares to pray for their dead. As with others, so here also there is in many cases but slender provision. And yet nowadays they cannot come to friends, but must needs hire a room and pay rent to a landlord. Nor can we venture to pass too harsh a verdict on the capitalist who evicts his tenant—though a woman and delicately nurtured—when the rent has fallen too long into arrears. For he probably has to deal with the fact on such a scale that the course is forced upon him, if he will save himself from ruin. More striking even than this is that fear of the police, which we find everywhere amongst the helpless, and which drives the keeper of the apartment-house to dismiss its penniless inmates when near to death, lest he should afterwards be arraigned in court for having stolen their provision!

Prostrate, then, under the disintegrating touch of the Modern Era, lies at this moment the most perfect of mediæval cities. Is she to become a memory to her children after four thousand or more years of a constant growth? Or will there prove to be some magic in the new forces of enthusiasm that are running through the veins of the nation, that shall yet make itself potent to renew her ancient life-streams also?

THE END